ALSO BY ANDREA WARREN

Charles Dickens and the Street Children of London

Escape from Saigon: How a Vietnam War Orphan Became an American Boy

Orphan Train Rider: One Boy's True Story

Pioneer Girl: A True Story of Growing Up on the Prairie

Surviving Hitler: A Boy in the Nazi Death Camps

The Boy Who Became Buffalo Bill: Growing Up Billy Cody in Bleeding Kansas

Under Siege!: Three Children at the Civil War Battle for Vicksburg

We Rode the Orphan Trains

The future U.S. secretary of transportation as a toddler.

ENEMY CHILD

The Story of Norman Mineta, a Boy Imprisoned
in a Japanese American Internment Camp
During World War II

Andrea Warren

MARGARET FERGUSON BOOKS
HOLIDAY HOUSE · NEW YORK

The publisher wishes to thank Dakota Russell, museum manager at Heart Mountain Interpretive Center; Professor Yoon Pak of the University of Illinois; and Steve Rabson, professor emeritus of East Asian Studies at Brown University for their expert reviews of the text.

MARGARET FERGUSON BOOKS

Unless otherwise noted, internment camp photos were taken at Heart Mountain.

Printed and bound in November 2018 at Toppan Leefung, DongGuan City, China.

www.holidayhouse.com

First Edition

1 3 5 7 9 10 8 6 4 2

Library of Congress Cataloging-in-Publication Data
Names: Warren, Andrea, author.
Title: Enemy child : the story of Norman Mineta, a boy imprisoned in a
Japanese American internment camp during World War II / Andrea Warren.
Description: First edition. | New York, NY : Margaret Ferguson Books/Holiday
House, [2019] | Audience: 4–6. | Audience: 10+ | Summary: "A biography of
Norman Mineta, from his internment as a child in Heart Mountain Internment
Camp during World War II, through his political career including serving
in congress for ten terms during which time he was instrumental in getting
the Civil Liberties Act of 1988 passed which provided reparations and an
apology to those who were interned"— Provided by publisher. | Includes
bibliographical references and index.
Identifiers: LCCN 2018009814 | ISBN 9780823441518 (hardcover)
Subjects: LCSH: Mineta, Norman Yoshio, 1931—Juvenile literature.
Legislators—United States—Biography—Juvenile literature. | Japanese
Americans—Evacuation and relocation,
1942–1945—Children—Biography—Juvenile literature. | World War,
1939–1945—Children—United States—Biography—Juvenile literature. |
World War, 1939–1945—Japanese Americans—Children—Biography—Juvenile
literature. | Heart Mountain Relocation Center
(Wyo.)—Children—Biography—Juvenile literature. | LCGFT: Biographies.
Classification: LCC D769.8.A6 W37 2019 | DDC 940.53/1773092 [B]—dc23
LC record available at https://lccn.loc.gov/2018009814

For Jack. Welcome, little one.

CONTENTS

"I want my children to understand in their bones what happened to their grandma and grandpa, and to pass that knowledge on to their children so that it doesn't happen again."

BARBARA YASUI, DAUGHTER OF HEART MOUNTAIN
AND TULE LAKE INTERNEES

"Only what we could carry was the rule, so we carried Strength, Dignity, and Soul."

—LAWSON FUSAO INADA, POET INTERNED AT JEROME
AND AMACHE INTERNMENT CAMPS

Introduction

I first saw Heart Mountain on a cloudless September afternoon in 2014. I was in Cody, Wyoming, to visit Yellowstone National Park, and learned that an interpretive center had just opened nearby at the former Heart Mountain War Relocation Center.

I was immediately curious. I knew that the government had said it was necessary to send Japanese Americans to internment camps during World War II, but what had that experience been like for them? I decided to visit.

On the thirteen-mile drive to the site of the camp, I saw Heart Mountain gradually coming into view. By the time I arrived, the mountain dominated the horizon.

The interpretive center's displays told the story of the camp and its ten thousand internees. As I learned about their daily lives—the crowded barracks, bad food, endless lines to use communal restrooms, and suffering caused by weather that was dry, dusty, windy, and sometimes as cold as thirty degrees below zero—I could only shake my head that this had happened to them.

Their crime? Quite simply, they looked like the enemy. In 1942, America was at war with Japan. Fearing a Japanese invasion of the West Coast, the government imprisoned 120,000 Japanese Americans who lived along the coast so they could not collaborate with possible enemy invaders.

These people were persecuted, prosecuted, their businesses shut down, and their bank accounts frozen. They were registered, rounded up, put aboard trains and buses to unknown destinations, and kept behind barbed wire in ten different camps, all primitive and hastily built and all located in isolated, inhospitable, semi-populated areas far from public view. They were never found guilty of anything—or even charged with anything—yet they were treated like criminals because of their Japanese ancestry.

Even while imprisoned, most Japanese Americans remained patriots. They saluted the flag, raised money for the Red Cross, and knitted warm socks for American soldiers. When their sons were finally allowed to join the military, these young men became one of the most heroic fighting forces in our history and helped defeat both Germany and Japan.

I decided I wanted to write about this dark chapter of American history. I am most fortunate that Norman Mineta, a distinguished statesman and a ten-term member of Congress who also served in two presidential Cabinets, allowed me to tell his story of growing up Japanese American and his family's internment at Heart Mountain. As you read this book, I hope you will envision yourself in his shoes—a boy bewildered by Pearl Harbor, shamed by classmates who saw him as the enemy, worried for the safety of his parents, and finally forced from his home.

In large part because of Norman Mineta's work in Congress, the American government admitted its mistake and apologized for what it had done to Japanese Americans. And yet we still single out certain groups for discrimination. As one example, Muslim Americans are sometimes targeted because they share a religion with small groups of violent extremists. We are a nation of immigrants, yet we are still often hostile to those seeking new lives in America.

The story of what this country did to our Japanese Americans can teach us the injustice of such actions and inspire us to find compassionate solutions. As Norman Mineta knows firsthand, hate and exclusion are not the answers.

CHAPTER 1

Before the Storm

All nine-year-old Norman Mineta wanted to do every day after school was play baseball. It was the fall of 1941, and California's blue skies and the baseball field beckoned.

Instead, his parents insisted that he go to Japanese language class. Five days a week, he and other Japanese American boys and girls from his neighborhood in San Jose met in a room at the Buddhist church for the hour-long class.

Norm dreaded it. The Japanese alphabet was torture. Trying to memorize it made his head spin. He wasn't fluent like his parents, but he could speak some Japanese because he'd grown up with it, so why did it matter if he ever learned how to read and write it? English was his language and the only one he cared about. A glance in the mirror might remind him of his Japanese heritage, but he was all American.

He had never met his grandparents, aunts, uncles, and cousins living in Japan. His parents stayed in close touch with them through letters—all written in Japanese, of course. Norm had white friends whose grandparents lived close by, and he supposed it would be nice if his did, too. But most of his Japanese American friends were like him, with their grandparents back in the old country.

Still, he had plenty of family: Mama, Papa, his three older sisters, and his older brother. And they got together regularly with the Kimura family and other friends for birthday parties, ball games, holidays, and movie outings. "They were our extended family," Norm said. "We were at each other's houses all the time. We took turns hosting Easter, Thanksgiving, and Christmas, but the Fourth of July was always a cookout in our backyard around the brick barbecue pit that Papa had built."

Because the parents of these families had been born in Japan, they were known as Issei *(Ee-say)*, meaning first generation. Norm and all of the other children had been born in America and were Nisei *(Nee-say)*—second generation. The families lived in an area of San Jose known as Japantown. It had its own stores, businesses, and churches, and was home to several thousand Japanese Americans. Nearby were Filipino American and Chinese American communities. Norm's father had his own business, the Mineta Insurance Agency.

As American as their lives were, Norm understood his parents' emotional ties to their homeland. Three years before his birth, Papa and Mama had taken his sisters and brother to visit family in Japan. Growing up, Norm had seen small, grainy photos from this trip. One was of a six-year-old boy in a white sailor suit—his brother, Albert, staring solemnly at the camera.

Norm sensed that this visit had been very important for his parents, particularly Papa. In Japan the father was accorded great respect as head of the family. Papa wanted his relatives to see that even though he lived in America, he was an honorable Japanese family man. When each of his children was born, he followed ancient custom, seeing to it that the announcement of the birth was relayed to the Buddhist temple in Japan where relatives from both sides of the family still worshipped, exactly as their ancestors had done. Norm's birth was recorded in the family's official registry at the temple: Norman Yoshio Mineta, born November 12, 1931.

In other ways, Papa was fully Americanized. Unlike most Issei, he spoke excellent English. Mama struggled to read and write English and had a heavy accent. "She always called me 'No-man' because like many Japanese raised in Japan she had trouble pronouncing the letter *r*," Norm said. "I thought of it as her special name for me, even though I knew she couldn't help the way she said it."

Like her husband and children, Mama readily blended the new with the old. Sometimes the Minetas used silverware, but mostly they preferred chopsticks, even to eat chicken casserole, beef stew, and other American favorites that they enjoyed as much as Mama's Japanese specialties like sukiyaki, udon noodles, and spicy tofu.

Norm as an infant.

Norm thought of himself as the caboose of the family. His sister Aya (*Eye-ya*), who was serious and smart, was sixteen years older than he. Etsu, the fun sister who loved to laugh and joke, was fifteen years older. Helen was twelve years older; she was the peacemaker, the one who always made sure everyone was okay. Albert, who was quiet and shy and usually had his nose in a book, was eight years older. "I was so much younger that I did not share a childhood with my siblings. I only really knew them as adults," Norm said. "They took very good care of me when I was little. I was spoiled."

Each of Norm's siblings was an excellent student and a dutiful child. Albert planned to be a doctor, and Norm's sisters

This 1935 photo was taken in front of the Minetas' home. Back row: Helen, Etsu, and Aya. Front row: Albert, Norm, and their parents.

were all college educated. "Issei friends questioned why my parents would send my sisters to college, for this was uncommon in Japanese families, both in Japan and here in America," Norm said. "But Papa wanted to ensure that his daughters never had to do field work to put food on the table. He said college degrees would help them take advantage of the opportunities America offered. At the same time, their studies included secretarial courses because jobs could be limited for women—and especially for Asian women—and there were always openings for good secretaries."

With such strong role models, Norm had much to live up to. He tried not to complain about having to go to Japanese language class. He also had a weekly violin lesson, which he dreaded. He went only to please Mama and because Papa had bought a violin for him and expected him to do his best to learn it. "When I practiced, my playing sounded like loud screeching," Norm said. "I never got better, and I don't know how my family stood it."

Most of Norm's classmates at Jefferson Grammar School were white, but he also had Asian classmates who were Japanese, Chinese, Korean, or Filipino. Their fathers, like Norm's, had come to the United States to labor in California's agricultural fields, and many still did. There were also a few African American and Hispanic classmates.

Norm took his lunch to school each day and sat with friends of all different ethnic backgrounds while they ate their sack lunches. Sometimes he brought bologna or peanut butter and jelly sandwiches, and sometimes he brought his favorite rice rolls. "None of us thought anything of it," Norm said. "We kids easily accepted this cultural mix. At home in my neighborhood I played with my Japanese American friends. At school I had both Asian and other friends. It didn't matter."

School was hard for Norm—even harder than Japanese or violin lessons. When he tried to read, letters jumbled together. In math class, numbers reversed themselves. He spent long, frustrating hours on his studies, not daring to come home with a grade below a B. His parents and teachers insisted he wasn't working hard enough, and he blamed himself for his difficulties.

"I felt like a dummy. I'd tell myself, *You're stupid! You can't even write numbers down right!* Mama thought that if I just kept trying, in time I would overcome my problems. That never truly happened. School was a struggle for me."

Papa always told him, "Plan your work, and work your plan," so that's what Norm did. "I found that if I went very slowly, I could puzzle the letters into words. I was never formally diagnosed with dyslexia, but based on what we know now, I believe that was my problem. To this day, I read slowly, working out the words. If you give me a telephone number, I've trained myself to jot it down and then read it back several times to be certain I have the numbers in the right sequence."

Away from school and lessons, Norm played hard. He romped with his dog, Skippy, a mixed-breed stray that showed up one day at the Mineta home. Norm and his best friend, Eddie Kimura, often hung out with Tom Kitazawa, Richard Omishi, and Eddie's younger brother, John. The boys were baseball crazy. They improvised pickup games and begged their parents to take them to see San Jose's minor league team when it played, cheering loudly for the several Japanese American players. They loved other sports, too, and during football season Tom's sister, who was old enough to drive, would sometimes take them to football games at nearby Stanford University, which had a special section in the end zone just for kids.

There was something to do all the time and someone to do it with. The boys played marbles endlessly. Each had a baseball card collection and they regularly traded cards. Norm was always on the lookout for Chicago Cubs players, because the Cubbies were *his* team. The boys borrowed each other's comic books, especially favorites like Superman, Batman, and Green Lantern. They tuned in to *Captain Midnight* on the radio, listening for clues to help decipher coded messages with their Ovaltine decoder badges. Ovaltine, the show's sponsor, was a chocolate powder they mixed into milk. "To get a decoder, we had to send a certain number of Ovaltine labels to the company. So we all drank an awful lot of it," Norm said.

Sometimes the boys walked the ten blocks to downtown San Jose to see a movie, then headed to a nearby hot-dog stand to treat themselves to hot dogs smothered in onions. Norm was also an enthusiastic Cub Scout. "My uniform was my favorite outfit. I loved to wear it and was very proud of the badges I'd earned. My mother sewed each one on my shirt. No one ever had to force me to go to Scouts."

The only time Norm gave much thought to being Asian was when he experienced subtle discrimination. Usually it was in a store while waiting for help from a white clerk who assisted white customers first, even if they'd come in after Norm. He knew without being told

Norm and several buddies posed for a picture during the summer of 1941 on the steps of the Kimura home. Left to right: John Kimura, Norm, Eddie Kimura, and Richard Omishi.

not to say anything. It was just the way it was, and besides, most whites were nice. His sister Helen had thought about discrimination in a more serious way, however, for she wanted to be a teacher, and California schools did not hire Asians.

Because he was outgoing and talkative, but also polite and mannerly, Norm was well liked by everyone. He did what he was told. "My parents were strict and I rarely disobeyed them," he said. Although there was the one time that he, Eddie, Tom, Richard, and John took a cigar belonging to Mr. Kimura and smoked it under the Kimuras' front porch. "We would have been punished if we'd gotten caught. But we didn't like that cigar very much. I'm surprised none of us got sick."

It was Norm who had suggested the cigar. "I was usually the instigator. I was an imp and loved to tease."

His sister Etsu knew this well. She lived at home and worked at an art store. Her boyfriend, Mike Masaoka (*Ma-sah-o-ka*), lived in nearby San Francisco and visited on weekends. When they sat together in the living room to talk, Norm hid behind the sofa, knowing that Mike would give him a dime to go away. "I could be a real pest," Norm said. "One time I got a quarter because Mike didn't have any other change. That was a great day."

On Sundays Norm went to Sunday school at the Japanese Methodist Episcopal Church before attending the morning's service with his family. Whenever he went somewhere with his parents, he loved being seen with his stylish mother. "Mama dressed very nicely in the latest fashions, and she always wore a hat and gloves," Norm said. "She was careful of how much she spent on clothes, although she didn't need to worry about that."

Indeed, the Minetas were well enough off that they took road trips each summer, visiting places like Yosemite National Park, the Grand

Canyon, and Lake Tahoe. Apart from summer vacations, Norm's favorite trip was to visit Aya at her apartment in San Francisco. She had earned a business degree from the University of California at Berkeley and worked as an assistant for an executive at a shipping firm.

Norm was proud that Aya had won the California State Spelling Bee in high school. "At the time, people couldn't get over a Japanese girl winning it," said Norm, "but Aya was actually an American who won it. She just happened to have Japanese ancestry."

In Europe and Asia, war was raging that fall of 1941. Norm paid little attention. He heard reports on the radio, and at the movies he saw newsreels of Adolf Hitler speaking at huge Nazi rallies, along with bombs falling from the sky and fleeing refugees. But it wasn't America's war and none of it had anything to do with him. He was busy with school, lessons, baseball, and friends, and he was looking forward to his tenth birthday in November.

"I believed that nothing bad could happen to me—that my parents would always take care of me," he said. "I took pride in their stories of coming to America. Papa, especially, had overcome many obstacles. He was my hero. In my eyes, he could do anything."

CHAPTER 2

Coming to America

Norm's papa, Kunisaku (*Ku-nee-saku*) Mineta, knew no English when he stepped off the boat in Seattle, Washington, in 1902. He was fourteen years old and, as an adventure, had come to visit his uncle who lived in America. In Japan the Minetas were farmers who grew tea and strawberries. Japanese society was built on strong rules, and tradition dictated that the eldest son in the family, who was Papa's older brother, would inherit the family property. Because of this, Papa was unsure of what he wanted to do with his life. He hoped seeing something of the world would help him figure it out.

His uncle was also a younger son who would never inherit land of his own. He had immigrated to America several years earlier and lived in Salinas, south of San Francisco, where he worked in the agricultural fields. He had written home to suggest that one of his nephews come visit to observe American farming practices. Papa wanted to go.

Not understanding how large the United States was, Papa mistakenly booked his passage to Seattle instead of to San Francisco. The two cities were eight hundred miles apart. He had arrived with no money, and it took him two years to reach his uncle, working in lumber camps and on farms along the way. He often labored alongside fellow Asians who had come to America to escape poverty and lack of jobs at home. Agricultural work was especially plentiful in California, and Asians were willing to work longer hours at lower wages than most white workers.

His uncle advised Papa to become fluent in English so he could

Japanese immigrant laborers sort berries into boxes on a fruit farm in California around 1912.

be more than a field hand. The best way, said his uncle, was to attend public school, which was free. Even though he was now sixteen, Papa was soon in class, seated next to young children. When he left a year later, he had mastered English. This skill would be his ticket to success in America. He hired out to help harvest sugar beets and other vegetables around Salinas, and with his knowledge of English, he soon became one of the supervisors. When his uncle decided to move back to Japan, Papa assumed he would also return someday, for he knew that in this country he would always be a second-class American.

Since the early nineteenth century, Asian immigrants from China, Japan, Korea, and the Philippines had come to America seeking work. They were often discriminated against by Americans fearing for their own jobs.

Chinese immigrants had flooded into California in the 1840s to participate in the gold rush and to help build the railroads. In an effort to protect the jobs of American workers, the government first restricted how many Chinese could enter the country and then enacted the Chinese Exclusion Act of 1882, which halted Chinese immigration for the next twenty years. In 1902 the law was made permanent. This was the first time in American history that the government restricted immigration from a specific country.

Japanese workers were next to be targeted. In 1907, five years after Papa's arrival, America and Japan jointly ended the immigration of Japanese workers in what was known as the Gentlemen's Agreement. However, family members were allowed to join Japanese immigrants already in the States. This included tens of thousands of Japanese women and children who were able to reunite with their husbands and fathers, and brides with their bridegrooms.

Papa decided to stay in America in spite of its blatant racism. He

During the gold rush of the 1840s and '50s, some Chinese immigrants mined for gold on their own, while others, like the immigrants in this photo, worked with or for other miners.

loved California's mild climate and rich soil. With his knowledge of English, he had a good future, filled with work opportunities. Just as important, no one told him how to think or act or what his social obligations were, as they would have in Japan. Here, he was his own man.

In 1912, when Papa was twenty-four and had money saved, he felt it was time to marry and start a family. His heart's desire was a traditional Japanese bride. One option was to take his chances with a "picture bride"—a Japanese practice in which an intermediary or matchmaker selected a prospective wife. Many men working outside Japan preferred brides from home, and women who signed up to be picture brides wanted to escape poverty and hunger, start over some-where else, or experience adventure. Introduced through the mail

These picture brides arriving at Angel Island in California in 1910 preferred traveling as a group. They offered one another friendship and comfort on the journey to a new land and a new life.

by the intermediary, the couple exchanged photos and letters, and if both agreed, the bride's name was entered into the husband's family registry, legalizing their marriage in Japan. The bridegroom paid the young woman's passage by ship to America and met her at the dock, and they were immediately married in an American ceremony since the U.S. government did not consider their Japanese marriage to be valid.

Sometimes these unions worked out well. Other times, the couple never settled into a happy marriage. Either one or both parties might have misrepresented themselves by sending photos that showed them at a younger age or that were of someone else entirely. Perhaps a woman would claim skills that she did not possess, or a man might say he had a better job than he actually did. Papa had heard these stories and wanted to be careful.

He wrote to a boyhood friend, asking him to serve as a matchmaker and select several appropriate young women who were willing to cross the ocean to marry a stranger. By return mail came photos and introductions. His friend also included a photo of his younger sister, Kane (*Kah-neh*), who was now twenty years old and was from Papa's hometown of Mishima. Papa remembered her as a little girl and how he used to tease her. He knew immediately that she was right for him. The two families were friends, and Papa was confident they would approve of the match so he responded, "I'd be honored to marry her."

Kane, who would become Norm's Mama, arrived in San Francisco in January 1914, and they quickly got married. To Papa's delight,

These photos of Norm's parents were part of the official documentation necessary for Mama's immigration and their marriage. Mama's was taken in Japan.

they hit it off immediately. She remembered Papa from her child-hood—perhaps she'd even had a crush on him. Mama had attended a Christian grammar school founded by Methodist missionaries and had been a Methodist ever since. Papa soon converted from Bud-dhism to Mama's religion.

Their arranged marriage thrived. They settled in Salinas, and Mama helped in the sugar-beet fields where Papa was a supervisor. When Papa got a job helping to run a sugar-beet farm just south of

Norm believes this photo was taken shortly after his parents' marriage in 1914. Mama had readily adopted the dress style of her new country but enjoyed wearing traditional kimonos for special occasions.

San Jose, they moved there. San Jose had thirty thousand residents at the time, and only three hundred were Asian.

In 1913, a year before Mama's arrival, Califor-nia passed laws forbidding all Asian immigrants from owning land or becoming citizens and vot-ing. Even so, Mama loved America, and she was as frustrated as Papa by this. Their consolati-on was that their children born here would automati-cally be American citizens and have those rights as guaranteed under the Constitution. They wel-comed their daughters Aya in 1915, Etsu in 1916, and Helen in 1919.

When Helen was a baby, Papa came down with the flu and was in the Santa Clara County Hospital for nearly five months recovering. He had contracted Spanish influenza, the cause of a worldwide epidemic that killed millions of peo-ple. He was lucky to have survived.

But he was permanently weakened and could never again do strenuous labor; his work in agri-culture was over. To support his family he took whatever odd jobs he could find, including serving as a court interpreter, work he got because of his fluency in both Japanese and English. One day two white businessmen introduced themselves as executives of the West Coast Life Insurance Company, headquartered in San Francisco. They had heard about Papa's language skills and were seeking a bilingual independent agent in San Jose who could sell their insurance to Japanese clients. If Papa would do this, they would teach him the insurance business so he could start his own company.

Papa realized that this was a golden opportunity for him. The business he started, the Mineta Insurance Agency, represented the West Coast Life Insurance Company. Later he added auto and health insurance to his offerings. It was highly unusual at the time for an Issei to become an independent businessman, and that was one reason Papa was soon a respected leader of the San Jose Japanese American community.

In 1928, now the father not only of three daughters but also of Albert, who was born in 1923, Papa set out to build a home and office in San Jose. Since California law prevented Asians from owning land, a white lawyer named J. B. Peckham, who strongly disagreed with this law, put the property in his own name. He did the same for many other Asian immigrants. When Aya turned twenty-one and could legally own property, the title was transferred to her. This ensured that the home stayed in the Mineta family.

Norm grew up in that house. He always loved that the front porch had two doors: one led into the house and the other into Papa's office. The house was located across the street from the Japanese Methodist Episcopal Church, where they were members. As a little boy, every Saturday Norm would accompany his father to the savings and loan that held the mortgage on their house to make a payment of $32.48.

At the start of December 1941, the Mineta family looked forward to a happy future. In addition to running his business, Papa was friends with San Jose officials and businessmen, and because of his excellent English, he often served as a liaison between the city and its growing Japanese American community.

Mama was the heart of the home, lovingly caring for her family. Aya was in San Francisco, and Etsu, Helen, and Albert still lived at home. Etsu had her job at the art store. Helen was a secretary at San Jose State College, where Albert was a sophomore in the premed program. And Norm, who had just turned ten, was a Cub Scout and a busy fourth grader at Jefferson Grammar School.

Then, on December 7, came Pearl Harbor.

The Mineta home in San Jose was one of the first stucco houses in the area. The front door on the right led into Papa's office, and the other into the family's living room.

CHAPTER 3

War at Home

When church let out and Norm and his parents crossed the street to their home shortly after noon on December 7, neighbors were waiting outside for them. From inside the house Norm heard the phone ringing nonstop.

The news was devastating: early that morning Japan had bombed the United States naval base at Pearl Harbor, Hawaii, severely damaging the Pacific Fleet's ships and planes. Casualties were thought to be in the thousands.

"Papa immediately turned on the radio to hear news updates and he kept it on the rest of the day," Norm said. "People often brought their concerns to my father, and they looked to him now to help make sense of what was happening. They were dismayed that Japan would do something so terrible and wondered what it meant for them. Surely, they said, no one would think that they had anything to do with the attack, for they were loyal only to the American flag. But Papa told them that they should be concerned."

Relations between the U.S. and Japan had been strained for a long time. Japan felt insulted by the discrimination suffered by Issei in America. In addition to the previous anti-Asian laws, the Immigration Act of 1924 had set immigration quotas on certain countries and permanently ended immigration from Japan and other Asian countries. Then, just a year before Pearl Harbor, the Alien Registration Act of 1940 added further insult, requiring all alien residents over the age of fourteen to be photographed and fingerprinted and to register every year with the government. It would not be until the early 1950s that all of the anti-Asian laws would be repealed.

Far more important was the clash between the two countries over

The USS *Shaw*, shown here, was one of eight battleships at Pearl Harbor that either sank or was badly damaged. "Remember Pearl Harbor!" became the American military's battle cry.

Japan's relentless military expansion in Asia and the menace it posed to a number of Pacific islands that were U.S. territories. These included Guam, Wake Island, and the Philippines, where there were American air and naval bases. Certain that America would respond with military action to its aggressive advances, Japanese leaders had decided to strike first and attack Pearl Harbor. They gambled that they would damage America's fighting power so severely that it would no longer be a threat.

Japan had already forged an alliance with Hitler's Germany, and while America was not yet at war with Germany, few doubted it soon would be. Surely America could not fight wars in both Europe and the Pacific Ocean, especially with its Pacific Fleet crippled. Without American opposition, Japan could continue to take over strategic Pacific islands.

Norm hadn't paid attention to relations between America and Japan—that was something for grown-ups—but he knew that day by the worried voices around him that the bombing of Pearl Harbor meant something very significant had just happened.

"The men went inside Papa's office and closed the door to talk, while the women joined my mother in the kitchen," Norm said. "The door to Papa's office from the inside hallway was glass and covered with a curtain. I sat pressed against it, trying to hear what the men were saying. By now we knew that the Japanese had also attacked Wake Island."

Suddenly the back screen door burst open and the young daughter of the Hirano family next door ran into the house. "They're taking Papa away!" she cried. "They're taking him away!"

Norm followed as his father raced next door. But Mr. Hirano was already gone and his horrified family did not know who the men were who had handcuffed him, forced him into a car, and driven off.

"Papa called the city manager of San Jose to ask what was going on," Norm said. "The city manager had no idea. Then Papa called the chief of police, who also knew nothing, but suggested my father contact the sheriff. The sheriff said, 'Mr. Mineta, it's the FBI who did this, it's not any of the rest of us. I'll have them call you and explain.'"

Instead, late that afternoon an FBI agent arrived at the Mineta home. Once again, Norm stayed close, listening. "The agent told my father that they were picking up people who were community leaders or might be collaborating with the Japanese to invade the United States. Mr. Hirano was the executive director of the Japanese Association in San Jose. It was only a social organization for Issei and their families. My father told the agent that he was also a member and that Mr. Hirano was loyal to America. The agent had no information about where Mr. Hirano had been taken or when he might come home."

Norm was breathless with fear that his father would be next. "I was very afraid. What would my family do if the FBI arrested him?"

That evening he watched anxiously as Papa packed a suitcase. He wanted to be ready if the FBI arrested him. "When no one came, we were very relieved, but I think my father felt a little insulted," Norm said. "If they were arresting all the leaders, didn't they consider him important enough? They probably left him alone because he had so many influential white friends, including the president of San Jose State College, who sometimes came to our home for dinner."

For Americans with Japanese ancestry, Pearl Harbor was the beginning of a nightmare. Over 2,300 U.S. soldiers and sailors died in Japan's attack, and another 1,100 were wounded. In addition to Wake Island, Guam and the Philippines had also been attacked, and Americans were furious. They were also fearful that the West Coast was now vulnerable to an invasion by Japan. Overnight, Japan became a despised enemy. Could Japanese Americans who lived along the West

Coast be trusted, or were they in collusion with the Japanese, aiding them from the inside?

This suspicion—this guilt by association—confused and distressed Norm. "I'd never thought of being Japanese American as something negative," he said. "But at school the day after it happened, several kids yelled at me, 'You bombed Pearl Harbor!' I wasn't the enemy, but since I looked like the enemy, I thought I must *be* the enemy—because they sure thought I was.

"In those early days after Pearl Harbor, for the first time in my life, I saw my father cry. He loved America and could not understand why the land of his birth had attacked the land of his heart."

CHAPTER 4

The World at War

Norm would always remember what happened next. On December 8, America and its ally Great Britain declared war on the Empire of Japan. The British, who were already at war with Germany and its ally Italy, also declared war on Japan because it had attacked several British colonies in Asia. Three days later, in a matter of hours, Germany and Italy declared war on America, and America declared war on them.

The two sides squared off. Japan, Germany, and Italy were the major Axis powers. America, Great Britain, France, and the Soviet Union were the major Allies. The world was at war.

In the United States, Americans became wary of anyone with Japanese, German, or Italian ancestry. Who was loyal to America? Who was working for the enemy? Within hours of the declaration of war against Germany and Italy, the FBI also began rounding up German and Italian Americans considered "suspicious." Of the thousands arrested, most had court hearings and were released. Those considered especially dangerous were imprisoned. The United States had a population of 133 million in 1941, and more than a third had German or Italian heritage. Most were well assimilated into American society—meaning they looked typically American. It would be impossible to detain tens of millions of them.

But for Japanese Americans, it was a very different story. No one feared an East Coast invasion by Germany or Italy, while a Japanese invasion of the West Coast seemed a real possibility. Already, Japanese submarines had been detected in coastal waters—and more than 120,000 of America's 150,000 Japanese Americans lived within fifty miles of the coast in California, Oregon, and Washington.

Theodor Geisel, better known as Dr. Seuss, caricatured all Japanese Americans as treasonous in this February 1942 cartoon. The "5th Column" refers to people helping the enemy.

Months before the war began, when diplomatic relations between Japan and America had started to deteriorate, the FBI had begun compiling lists of Japanese Americans who were either community leaders or might support Japan.

It wasn't difficult to find them. They stood out because of their Japanese names and appearance, because many Issei still spoke Japanese, and because many were practicing Buddhists. Also, like other immigrant groups, immigrants from Japan and other Asian countries often formed their own communities and social organizations since they were not always welcomed into mainstream America.

These lists made it possible for FBI agents to swoop in just hours after Pearl Harbor was bombed. More than two thousand Japanese Americans, almost all of them on the West Coast, were arrested in the next eight weeks, including the Minetas' neighbor Mr. Hirano.

Sometimes FBI agents burst through closed doors, guns drawn, throwing their intended targets to the floor and handcuffing them before dragging them away. Suspects included farmers, fishermen, journalists, teachers, ministers, lawyers, businessmen, Japanese language teachers, martial arts instructors—anyone, male or female, in a leadership role or considered to be "pro-Japan." In San Jose they even came for the priest at the Buddhist church, and also for the Shinto priest, who was a woman. Somehow Norm's Japanese language teacher was spared, though classes never met again after Pearl Harbor, much to his relief.

Those picked up by the FBI were taken to local jails and then to prisons or detention centers, often far from home, without being allowed court hearings or to contact their families. Some families did not learn their loved ones' whereabouts for months. Many of these detainees were not released until the end of the war—even though they were never charged with espionage.

Norm's father did all he could to find out about Mr. Hirano, but it would be four months before the Hirano family learned that he had been sent 1,600 miles away to a Department of Justice prison in Bismarck, North Dakota. They would not be reunited with him for two years.

Over and over again, up and down the West Coast, Japanese Americans experienced the horror of FBI agents and police officers descending on their homes, confiscating anything from firecrackers to garden implements that they said could be useful to an invading enemy. Most Japanese Americans had always lived peacefully among

This family watches as an FBI agent searches their possessions, looking for anything suggesting loyalty to Japan.

their neighbors and could not understand why this was happening.

As rumors spread that Japan planned to invade the West Coast, many previously friendly neighbors grew hostile toward Japanese Americans. Some were beaten and tormented, and even had their houses and businesses firebombed. In the Little Tokyo district of Los Angeles, home to many of the city's thirty thousand Japanese Americans, carloads of whites terrorized the streets, yelling racial slurs, vandalizing businesses, and destroying fruit, vegetable, and flower stands. To save their own livelihoods, other Asian Americans scrambled to distance themselves from anyone with Japanese ancestry.

Some business owners even placed signs on their stores stating their ethnicity, hoping no one would think they were Japanese.

Norm felt the fallout at school. "My friend Larry Ng was Chinese American. He was afraid someone might think he was Japanese American, so every day he wore a pin that said 'I am a Chinese American.' He'd grin at me and say, 'I don't want to be rounded up with you guys and sent to some camp,' and I'd tease back, 'You look Japanese and I'm going to tell them to come get you.' We were already starting to hear rumors about camps, but we made jokes because we thought it *was* a joke."

Since Asian Americans were often lumped together by mainstream Americans, those who were not Japanese Americans tried to set themselves apart.

But as they would learn, international law sanctioned the imprisonment of "enemy aliens"—which meant noncitizens who were considered dangerous. Issei like Norm's parents, first-generation immigrants who had not been allowed to become American citizens, could therefore be confined to prison camps without being proven guilty of anything.

Norm knew that the Fifth Amendment to the Constitution guaranteed that "No person shall be deprived of life, liberty, or property without due process of law." He wondered if Nisei like him, who were born in America and were American citizens, would still have this protection. Knowing that his parents did not was very frightening.

Many Japanese Americans in other parts of the country suffered incidents of discrimination—mostly name-calling and vandalism to property—but it was nothing compared to what those on the West Coast experienced. Farmers were accused of planting their crops certain ways to guide invading enemy planes, and fishermen of using their shortwave radios to send signals to Japanese submarines. More than once, media outlets mistakenly reported that Los Angeles and San Francisco were under attack. With most of their leaders already arrested, the Japanese American community had difficulty responding to false rumors and allegations.

Norm started paying close attention to news on the radio and in the newspapers. Some stories were disturbing. *Time* magazine ran an article titled "How to Tell Your Friends from the Japs," and the *Los Angeles Times* proclaimed, "A viper is nonetheless a viper wherever the egg is hatched, so a Japanese-American, born of Japanese parents, grows up to be Japanese, not an American."

San Jose had several incidents of vandalism against Japanese Americans, but the city remained calmer than many places. "Our newspaper was cautioning people not to do anything vengeful,"

Norm said. "The editor reminded everyone that 'these are our friends and neighbors.'"

Eleanor Roosevelt, the wife of President Franklin Roosevelt, tried to deliver the same message. She visited the West Coast right after Pearl Harbor and had her photo taken with Japanese Americans.

In her syndicated newspaper column, "My Day," which appeared six days a week in ninety newspapers across the country, she warned people about unfair treatment of loyal Japanese, German, and Italian Americans, writing that they "must not feel they have suddenly ceased to be Americans."

Along with German and Italian Americans, Japanese Americans did all they could to show their loyalty and their love for America. They wrote letters of support to President Roosevelt and donated blood to the Red Cross. At the start of the war, three thousand Japanese Americans were already serving in the armed forces. Now young Nisei men lined up at recruiting stations, full of patriotism and eager to serve.

Community air-raid drills became part of civil defense preparation, and Japanese Americans practiced along with everyone else. If enemy planes invaded U.S. airspace, sirens would give warning for people to block any light visible from the air. Streetlights and car headlights had to be turned off, and everyone was told to get inside and cover their windows with blackout drapes.

But Japanese Americans faced ever-increasing hostility. Many lost their jobs. The Seattle school district fired its Japanese American teachers and at least one white teacher who was married to a Japanese American. Those who were dating people of other races either broke up or they quickly married, determined to endure together whatever happened next.

CHAPTER 5

Lowering the Net

In January 1942, the Japanese forces won victory after victory in the South Pacific, sinking American ships and downing aircraft, fueling the ever-increasing death toll of young men in the military.

The label "Jap" became a hateful racial slur used to describe both the enemy and Japanese Americans. At school, Norm started hearing it. Someone would say, "Hey, Jap," or "You dropped your pencil, Jap." The word cut deeply. He'd always grin like he thought they were joking, but inside he burned with shame.

Everyday life grew more difficult for Japanese Americans living on the West Coast. The government imposed travel restrictions, with police permission required for trips longer than five miles. Next came a curfew from 8 p.m. to 6 a.m.

Norm's sister Aya was getting married in San Francisco to her college sweetheart, Min Endo, who worked in his father's silk business, and all the family wanted to be there. Papa had to apply for a special permit since the trip was more than five miles, and he was given permission for only five people to go.

"So Albert stayed home," Norm said. "Etsu, Helen, and I were in the backseat as we drove to the city in the morning. We had a wonderful day but were a little late in leaving to return home. Mama was calm, but Papa got very nervous as curfew drew near. He started to speed—something he never did because he was so law abiding. He had me looking out the back window, watching for the police. By the time we reached home at a quarter past eight, we were all shaking."

Norm and his friend Eddie quit going to movies, even matinees. "It didn't feel right. Life seemed too serious to have fun," Norm said. "We stayed close to home. We would ask each other, 'What are your parents saying? What do you hear?' Our parents were trying to act like everything was okay. It's part of Japanese culture to bear one's problems with fortitude and without burdening others. I felt I shouldn't talk about my worries. For my parents' sake, I had to pretend that I was strong. I spent a lot of time playing with my dog Skippy, who seemed to understand my feelings."

And still things grew worse. The FBI continued to search homes looking for photos, letters, documents—anything suggesting loyalty to Japan. Agents confiscated radios, cameras, binoculars, Japanese ceremonial swords—whatever they thought could somehow be useful to the enemy during an invasion. When one Japanese American in the Seattle area read that shortwave radios were to be turned in to authorities, he tried two different times to give his to the local police, but they had no interest in it. Determined to follow the law, he left the radio at the police station in the middle of the night and then ran home.

Because of the searches, some frantic families burned picture albums, letters, gifts from grandparents, and items with Japanese writing on them. Others destroyed heirloom silk kimonos, tea sets, and other family treasures. At the Mineta home, Papa built a fire in the fireplace. Then, piece by piece, the family burned all the saved letters

An FBI agent checks radios voluntarily surrendered by Japanese Americans.

and photos from their Japanese relatives. Norm could tell how painful this was for his parents, but it had to be done. They debated what to do about several prized belongings they had acquired in Japan. "We had some beautiful lacquered trays that Mama used when we had special company," said Norm, "and two large antique vases that were over a hundred and fifty years old. We decided to risk keeping them, hoping they wouldn't be taken from us."

Although Albert wanted to finish college before serving in the military, he was very patriotic and was ready to go fight if he was drafted. But one afternoon in January, Norm came into the bedroom they shared and found his big brother visibly upset. "He showed me the letter he'd just received from the draft board," Norm said. "His status had been changed from 1-A—'ready, fit, and able to serve'—to 4-C: 'enemy alien.'

"Albert wasn't an alien since he was born in America," said Norm, "so why would they use this term? He wanted to serve his country, but his country was rejecting him."

Not only were Nisei no longer being accepted into the military, most of those already serving were discharged or demoted. Those who stayed could not be stationed on the West Coast. Wherever they were sent, they were given low-level jobs and were excluded from combat training for fear that they might be loyal to Japan. The exception to this treatment was a group of Nisei soldiers who were fluent in Japanese. Their language skills would prove invaluable in the fight against Japan.

Shortly after Albert's bad news, Papa gathered the family in the living room for a meeting, minus Aya, who would hear about it later in a phone call. Norm was worried; Papa clearly had something important to say. Albert, Helen, and Etsu looked worried, too, and Mama, who was always the strong one, was fighting back tears. But Papa's voice was steady when he spoke. "We don't know what's going to happen to your mother and me. We're hearing that some of us who were born in Japan are being taken into custody and exchanged for American soldiers who have been captured by the Japanese."

A wave of fear shot through Norm. His parents could be sent to Japan? How could this be? Albert patted Norm's shoulder as Papa continued. "Whatever happens, you are to stick together and take care of each other. This house is your home. It is legally in Aya's name and can't be taken from you. As American citizens, you are protected by the Constitution."

Papa was always right, but Norm still worried. "No one knew what the future held, or how to be ready for it," he said.

Then came another blow. Papa had sent in his business license for renewal, and it came back stamped SUSPENDED FOR THE DURATION OF THE WAR. Without his license, Papa could not sell insurance. As he quickly learned, Japanese Americans were being forced to close their businesses. Some found padlocks on their stores and offices, put there by the FBI.

Many Japanese Americans in California did their banking with the American branches of Japanese-owned banks, and these accounts were frozen. Account holders were allowed to withdraw only $100 a month.

"My father had money in a Japanese-owned bank, but also kept money in an American bank, so we were okay," Norm said. "But many people had all their funds in a Japanese bank. Such a small monthly withdrawal left most of them unable to pay their bills, taxes, and mortgages."

All along the West Coast, Japanese American farmers had successful small farms, either leasing the land or with ownership in their children's names. Their farms in California were so productive that they grew more than half of the state's fruits and vegetables. If they could not pay their taxes, leasing fees, or mortgages, they would lose them. An executive with a prominent agricultural organization admitted that white farmers were eager for this to happen. "We're charged with wanting to get rid of the Japanese for selfish reasons," he said. "We might as well be honest. We do." Then he stated what few would say out loud, though many thought it: "It's a question of whether the white man lives on the Pacific Coast or the brown man."

According to Norm, "In spite of all this, Papa told us that things would work out. Whatever was done to us, he went along with it. He'd say, 'Look, we're at war. No one trusts us right now. Let's prove our loyalty to our country by cooperating.' So that's what we tried to do."

But when President Roosevelt signed Executive Order 9066 on February 19, 1942, the Japanese American community was suddenly in even more trouble.

CHAPTER 6

Losing Everything

Rumors had circulated since shortly after Pearl Harbor that the government might force Japanese Americans into internment camps for the duration of the war. At first they didn't believe it. This was America, they assured each other. Things like that didn't happen here. But President Roosevelt's Executive Order 9066 stated that "any or all people" could be removed from restricted military areas. As Japanese Americans knew too well, "any or all" referred to them.

"We could only wait to see what would happen next," Norm said.

At the beginning of March the government announced the formation of two restricted areas—Military Area 1 and Military Area 2. Military Area 1 included a strip of land from the coast to fifty or more miles inland in the states of California, Washington, and Oregon. Part of Arizona was also included. Both San Jose and San Francisco were in Military Area 1. Japanese Americans were urged to voluntarily move to Military Area 2, which included the remaining parts of California, Oregon, and Washington—or to move even farther inland.

The 120,000 Japanese Americans living in Military Area 1 agonized over what to do. As many as nine thousand hurriedly moved, most to Military Area 2. Finding places where they were welcome was difficult because of the anti-Japanese hostility found almost everywhere. The rest of them stayed put in Military Area 1.

"We didn't feel we could move," Norm said. "We had no place to go and we didn't want to be farther from Aya and Min in San Francisco."

Etsu's boyfriend, Mike, was the executive secretary of a national organization for Nisei called the Japanese American Citizens League. Mike had been arrested by the FBI right after Pearl Harbor. But he was released because in his position at the JACL he was encouraging Japanese Americans to cooperate with the government. JACL officials decided in March to close their San Francisco headquarters and relocate to Salt Lake City, Utah, seven hundred miles away.

Even though Etsu missed him, she was relieved that Mike was already far from either military area when the government abruptly changed its policy a few weeks later. Because so few people voluntarily left, it announced that whoever had resettled in other parts of the country could stay there, but those who had moved to Military Area 2 in California, along with all Japanese Americans still in Military Area 1, were now forbidden to leave. For their own safety, they were informed, they would soon be evacuated to assembly

President Roosevelt signed Executive Order 9066 just eleven weeks after Pearl Harbor. It is considered one of the worst violations of civil rights in American history.

centers and from there to relocation centers for the duration of the war.

"We were told this was to protect us, but we knew it was because so many Americans viewed us as the enemy," Norm said. "We had no idea what these assembly and relocation centers would be like. All we could do was hope for the best and to try to be cooperative."

As they quickly learned, evacuations had already begun. The first had occurred in late February on Terminal Island, just a ferry ride away from Los Angeles. Among the island's three thousand residents was a close-knit community of several hundred Japanese Americans,

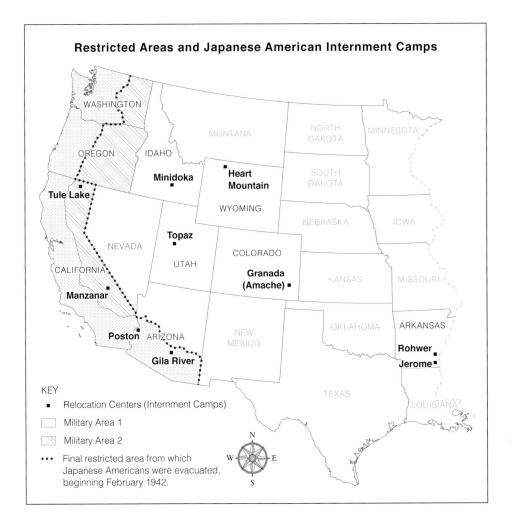

Restricted Areas and Japanese American Internment Camps

KEY

■   Relocation Centers (Internment Camps)

Military Area 1

Military Area 2

•••   Final restricted area from which Japanese Americans were evacuated, beginning February 1942.

Japanese Americans on Terminal Island lived in a thriving village in an area called Fish Harbor. Because their homes were destroyed, few would ever return.

most of them fishermen. After Pearl Harbor, there had been concern that they might be spies for Japan. With no proof, the government had given Japanese Americans just two days' notice before trucks arrived to take them away. Some had to be forced from their homes, which were later bulldozed. The Coast Guard confiscated most of their boats and fishing equipment. A community that had thrived for a hundred and fifty years simply vanished.

It was much different on Bainbridge Island, across Puget Sound from Seattle, Washington. When the three hundred Japanese American islanders were told to be ready to evacuate on March 30, neighbors jumped in to help. They offered to store their belongings and keep their farms running. One neighbor bought a family's farm for a dollar, pledging to resell it to them at that price after the war.

The general public saw Japanese Americans being rounded up for the first time when newspapers published photos like this one taken on Bainbridge Island.

Quakers—members of the Religious Society of Friends—who opposed war and felt that imprisoning Japanese Americans was wrong, looked after several of the farms. Islanders assured their Japanese American friends and neighbors that their property would be waiting for them upon their return.

On evacuation day, army trucks transported Japanese American families to the ferry for the crossing to Seattle, where a train awaited them. Dressed in their best and carrying their suitcases packed with as many belongings as they could fit, they walked with dignity to the docks. Islanders crowded around to say goodbye and share final hugs as they boarded the ferry, guarded by armed soldiers. When the evacuees reached Seattle, they were led by the soldiers to the waiting train, watched by hundreds of Seattle residents crowded onto an overpass, not all of them friendly. One Bainbridge evacuee recounted afterward that it was one of the most humiliating experiences of his life.

Up and down the coast that spring, government notices were posted in easy-to-see places a few days to a week before evacuation began for that area. They instructed male and female heads of households to report to centers set up by the Wartime Civil Control Administration to receive their evacuation instructions. Determined to prove their loyalty, they did whatever they were told to do. If cooperating with the government would help the war effort, they would do it.

San Francisco's Japanese Americans were evacuated during the month of April. Notices for Aya, Min, and his relatives were posted the last week of the month. Several days later they left for Tanforan

Obeying orders from the government, heads of families in San Francisco line up for processing, anxious to learn what they can about the coming evacuation.

Assembly Center, an hour south of San Francisco at the Tanforan Racetrack in San Bruno. Aya's first letter sounded upbeat. She reported little about their living conditions, causing Papa to speculate that she didn't want to alarm the family. She said that internees had no access to telephones, so communication must be by mail. Norm was jealous that his sister was now living at a racetrack. He hoped his family would be that lucky.

Every day, the Minetas awaited their orders. "Three thousand Japanese Americans lived in San Jose, and we were all on edge," Norm said. He continued going to school, and Albert attended his college

Arriving at Tanforan Racetrack, exhausted and confused internees tried to figure out where to go and what to do. Norm's sister Aya and her husband were sent to Tanforan.

New internees at Tanforan, hoping to make their barracks more livable, collected scrap lumber to build furniture.

classes. Helen still worked as a secretary, but Etsu had lost her job when her Japanese American employer was forced to close his art store, so she was home during the day with Mama and Papa.

And then, on May 23, the notices went up. Norm saw his first one posted on a light pole near home and learned that his family would be evacuated on May 30. They would be part of the last group to leave San Jose.

"Accepting that this was really happening was difficult," Norm said. "But at least we didn't have to wonder anymore *when* it was going to happen."

He read the entire announcement carefully. The heading was printed in large black type: INSTRUCTIONS TO ALL PERSONS OF JAPANESE ANCESTRY. One sentence stated, "All Japanese persons, both alien and non-alien, will be evacuated." Norm already knew this, and secretly he was glad, for he was terrified of being separated from his parents. But Papa, who was never wrong, was wrong about the Constitution protecting Nisei born in America.

The word "*alien*" still disturbed Norm, just as it had when he saw it on Albert's letter from the draft board. His context for the word was the space aliens he'd seen in comic books. They were typically grotesque, bright green creatures. Why couldn't the government just say *citizens* and *non-citizens* instead of *aliens* and *non-aliens*?

"These words made us feel like we were less than human, and that we deserved punishment," Norm said. "The military insisted that evacuation was meant to protect us, but even at my age I could see that being rounded up and sent away was wrong. Every single Issei and Nisei I knew was loyal to the American flag and wanted America to win the war in Europe and the Pacific."

The notice said that heads of households must report to a civil control station set up in the men's gym-

Evacuation notices were posted in visible areas like this one attached to a telephone pole in Sacramento, California. The evacuation notice below was posted in Norm's neighborhood in San Jose's Japantown.

WESTERN DEFENSE COMMAND AND FOURTH ARMY
WARTIME CIVIL CONTROL ADMINISTRATION

Presidio of San Francisco, California
May 23, 1942

INSTRUCTIONS
TO ALL PERSONS OF
JAPANESE
ANCESTRY

Living in the Following Area:

All of that portion of the County of Santa Clara, State of California, lying generally north and northwest of the following boundary: Beginning at the point on the Santa Cruz-Santa Clara County line, due west of a line drawn through the peak of Loma Prieta; thence due east along said line through said peak to its intersection with Llagas Creek; thence downstream along said creek toward Madrone to the point where it is crossed by Llagas Avenue; thence northeasterly on Llagas Avenue to U. S. Highway No. 101; thence northerly on said Highway No. 101 to Cochran Road; thence northeasterly on Cochran Road to its junction with Steeley Road; thence easterly on Steeley Road to Madrone Springs; thence along a line projected due east from Madrone Springs to its intersection with the Santa Clara-Stanislaus County line; together with all portions of Santa Clara County not previously covered by Exclusion Orders of this Headquarters.

Pursuant to the provisions of Civilian Exclusion Order No. 96, this Headquarters, dated May 23, 1942, all persons of Japanese ancestry, both alien and non-alien, will be evacuated from the above area by 12 o'clock noon, P. W. T., Saturday, May 30, 1942.

No Japanese person will be permitted to move into, or out of, the above area after 12 o'clock noon, P. W. T., Saturday, May 23, 1942, without obtaining special permission from the representative of the Commanding General, Northern California Sector, at the Civil Control Station located at:

Men's Gymnasium,
San Jose State College,
4th and San Carlos Streets,
San Jose, California.

Such permits will only be granted for the purpose of uniting members of a family, or in cases of grave emergency.

The Civil Control Station is equipped to assist the Japanese population affected by this evacuation in the following ways:

1. Give advice and instructions on the evacuation.
2. Provide services with respect to the management, leasing, sale, storage or other disposition of most kinds of property, such as real estate, business and professional equipment, household goods, boats, automobiles and livestock.
3. Provide temporary residence elsewhere for all Japanese in family groups.
4. Transport persons and a limited amount of clothing and equipment to their new residence.

The Following Instructions Must Be Observed:

1. A responsible member of each family, preferably the head of the family, or the person in whose name most of the property is held, and each individual living alone, will report to the Civil Control Station to receive further instructions. This must be done between 8:00 A. M. and 5:00 P. M. on Sunday, May 24, 1942, or between 8:00 A. M. and 5:00 P. M. on Monday, May 25, 1942.
2. Evacuees must carry with them on departure for the Assembly Center, the following property:
   (a) Bedding and linens (no mattress) for each member of the family;
   (b) Toilet articles for each member of the family;
   (c) Extra clothing for each member of the family;
   (d) Essential personal effects for each member of the family.
   All items carried will be securely packaged, tied and plainly marked with the name of the owner and numbered in accordance with instructions obtained at the Civil Control Station. The size and number of packages is limited to that which can be carried by the individual or family group.
3. No pets of any kind will be permitted.
4. No personal items and no household goods will be shipped to the Assembly Center.
5. The United States Government through its agencies will provide for the storage, at the sole risk of the owner, of the more substantial household items, such as iceboxes, washing machines, pianos and other heavy furniture. Cooking utensils and other small items will be accepted for storage if crated, packed and plainly marked with the name and address of the owner. Only one name and address will be used by a given family.
6. Each family, and individual living alone, will be furnished transportation to the Assembly Center. Private means of transportation will not be utilized. All instructions pertaining to the movement will be obtained at the Civil Control Station.

**Go to the Civil Control Station between the hours of 8:00 A. M. and 5:00 P. M.,
Sunday, May 24, 1942, or between the hours of 8:00 A. M. and 5:00 P. M.,
Monday, May 25, 1942, to receive further instructions.**

J. L. DeWITT
Lieutenant General, U. S. Army
Commanding

SEE CIVILIAN EXCLUSION ORDER NO. 96.

nasium at San Jose State College. They were to report there between the hours of 8:00 a.m. and 5:00 p.m., Sunday, May 24, 1942, or between the hours of 8:00 a.m. and 5:00 p.m., Monday, May 25, 1942, to receive further instructions.

Papa went to the control station the next day. He and others there were given details of when and where to go on the 30th, but not where the assembly center was that they and their families were being sent to. Aya and Min had gone to an assembly center close to home, but other people had been moved hundreds of miles away. Evacuees could bring only what they could carry, and this was to include bedding, towels, clothing, and essential personal effects.

This sign in a store in the Little Tokyo area of Los Angeles expressed the owners' affection for their loyal customers.

They were told that although Issei had already been photographed, fingerprinted, and registered because of the Alien Registration Act of 1940, the government now required all Japanese Americans to do this before they left, even children. It was a way to know who and where they were. They also had to be inoculated against communicable diseases.

"We had to get a bunch of shots," Norm said. "It was awful."

Papa was given tags printed with the Mineta family's assigned number: 130799. Tags were to be tied to each piece of luggage and also pinned to each person where they could be seen clearly during the evacuation.

When most people closed up their houses and businesses, they could only hope they would be okay.

Norm knew his family was fortunate, for they were able to rent their house to a college professor they knew. They left their furniture in place and put what belongings they could in the attic. They

Japanese Americans hurriedly sold their belongings for however much money they could get—and it was usually very little.

stored everything else at their church, including Mama's delicate china, her lacquered trays, and the antique vases. "I helped wrap each piece of china and pack all of it into boxes," Norm said. "We stored everything carefully, wondering if we'd ever see it again."

With nowhere to leave it, Papa decided he must sell the family's nearly new Packard automobile. Scavengers were coming through the neighborhood looking for bargains, and as their evacuation date quickly drew closer, Papa finally took an offer of $300 for the car, even though less than a year earlier he had paid $1,500 for it.

The hardest thing for Norm was giving up Skippy. "We couldn't bring pets with us. One day a guy who'd stopped to see if we had anything interesting to sell saw me playing with Skippy and said, 'Hey, what are you going to do with your dog?' I told him I didn't know. 'Can I have him?' he asked. He seemed nice and there was no time for me to find someone else to care for him . . . so I made Skippy go with him. It really tore me up. I felt sad about this for a long time.

"One good thing did happen. Papa gave my violin to the school music department. I was very glad, and hoped I'd never see another."

Packing was frustrating. Even with two large suitcases for each of them, there was too little room. Towels, sheets, shoes, everyday clothes, pajamas and robes, underwear, sweaters, books and personal items—they crammed in as much as they could. Norm somehow made room for his baseball card collection.

The day before evacuation, two FBI agents came to the house for a final check. "Papa was very polite, inviting them in and showing them around. We'd packed almost everything, so the house looked bare. I was relieved we'd already stored Mama's Japanese things so they couldn't question why we had them. They went from room to room, opening every drawer and closet. They also checked our packed luggage, looking for items like flashlights, cameras, or radios—things now considered illegal for us. They took Papa's camera, and that was the end of his taking family photos until he could get another one after the war. They also took Mama's iron because they said the camps didn't have enough electrical power for irons. Mama had always ironed everything—all our clothes, sheets and pillowcases and tablecloths. She was quite upset at losing it."

When it was time to go, the last thing the family did before leaving the house was to secure the tags with their assigned number to their suitcases and the clothes they were wearing. Until they reached the assembly center they would be known as Family No. 130799.

Ed and Betty Linderoth, old family friends, drove them to the train. Mama wore a stylish outfit, a hat, and high heels. Etsu and Helen had on nice dresses and heels. Papa wore his best suit and hat, and Albert his newest sweater and jacket. Norm had insisted on bringing his bat, ball, and glove, which he awkwardly carried, along with his suitcases. He had layered on as many pieces of clothing as he could. The last thing he put on was his Cub Scout uniform with all his badges. Not only was it his favorite outfit, but he had heard that on the train they let Cub Scouts and Boy Scouts serve as messengers.

"We were told that no one would be allowed to leave their train car," Norm said. "Some families would be split up in different cars, so if they wanted to send a message to each other, a messenger would deliver it. In spite of everything that was happening, I was very excited that I would be riding on the train overnight and that I would have this special job."

Instead of the train station, instructions said to report to the freight yard for departure. "Having to wear a number was bad enough. Now we were being made to feel second class, like we were no longer good enough to use the station," Norm said. "But in one way, it was okay. The freight yard was a few blocks from Jefferson Grammar School. We arrived during the noon lunch break and some of the kids had come to see us off. Eddie had left several days earlier, so I was glad a few of my classmates came, even though it was to say goodbye."

Armed MPs—military police—were everywhere, barking orders and keeping a close eye on everything happening. The Minetas stayed together, talking quietly to friends and neighbors. It took a long time to get everyone checked in. Norm felt like they had been waiting forever when one of the MPs walked over to him and

Once luggage was loaded, evacuees said final goodbyes to friends and boarded their train. Many felt overwhelmed by the reality of what was happening.

demanded he hand over his baseball bat because he could use it as a weapon.

Norm glanced at Papa, who nodded for him to do it. He fought down the lump in his throat as he made himself give his bat to the officer. It had been a gift from Papa and was one of his prized possessions. And now it was gone. He forced himself to stay quiet, but he felt angry.

After another long wait, they saw the train chugging toward them. At that same moment Norm realized that tears were rolling down his father's face. "I'd first seen Papa cry on Pearl Harbor Day, and now I saw his tears a second time. Suddenly I understood that this train was going to carry us away from our homes and everything we knew. We had already lost so much. We had no idea of what was going to happen to us, and we could do nothing to stop it."

It's hard to imagine that the government considered this little boy a threat. The elderly, disabled, and 17,000 children under the age of ten were among those sent to the camps.

CHAPTER 7

Santa Anita

Outside, the California sky was a sunny bright blue. Inside the train car, the light was dim. All the shades were drawn. Holding his ball and glove, Norm slid into a window seat and lifted the shade, hoping to wave a last goodbye to his friends. "Close it!" barked an MP. "No looking out!"

Papa took the seat next to Norm. "Do as you're told, Norman," he said quietly.

But why? Norm wondered. What could it possibly hurt to look through the window? First they took his bat, and now this.

MPs were stationed at the back and front of the car, their guns in plain view. They directed people into seats, warned them to not look outside, and reminded them that they were not allowed to leave the car.

But Norm could. He was going to deliver messages.

After what seemed like hours, everyone was finally settled and the train started to move. It was almost 5 p.m. The car grew quiet. Even the baby several rows back stopped fussing. Norm listened to the clickety-clack of the wheels and the sound of escaping steam as the train gathered speed. Then he realized he was hearing muffled sobs from some of the adults around him. He glanced across the aisle at Mama, but her face was turned away from him. Etsu sat by her and was patting her back. Helen and Albert were in the row behind Norm and Papa. Albert didn't say anything, but Helen was trying to cheer up Papa, who looked so sad that Norm feared he would cry again.

Once the train was rolling along, small children started playing games and Norm could hear their laughter. Every seat in the car was taken. You could stretch in your seat, but the only way to move a bit was to walk along the aisle and stop to visit with someone for a moment or two, or to get in line for the bathroom. Norm wished he could pull up his shade and watch the countryside go by. Several other people had tried to get a glimpse, and they, too, had been ordered to stop.

The train was heading south. Officials had not announced a destination, but people around Norm speculated that they were going to Santa Anita, a racetrack in Arcadia, near Los Angeles. They'd heard rumors that earlier evacuees from San Jose had already been taken there, so maybe that was where Eddie was. The legendary racehorse Seabiscuit, had won important races at Santa Anita. Norm thought that just *being* at that fabled racetrack would be exciting. Aya might even be jealous since it was more famous than Tanforan Racetrack.

It had been in the news that the government had quickly prepared fifteen temporary assembly centers along the West Coast to house Japanese Americans until the permanent camps were ready— although some had already been sent directly to a couple of the camps, even though they were not yet finished. Most of the assembly centers were at racetracks or fairgrounds—large facilities that could be easily guarded and already had water and electricity. Animal stables were being turned into housing, and primitive barracks were being hastily constructed for the overflow. Norm didn't worry about that. He was just excited that they were very possibly going to the greatest racetrack of them all. Now, if only Eddie was there!

The hours passed slowly as the train lumbered along. The family snacked on the large bag of rice rolls and drank the tea that Mama had brought. Norm wished he could play cards with Albert—other people in the car were playing cards—but Mama had never allowed card playing or dancing. Even more evil were smoking and drinking. She was a strict Methodist in that way.

When an MP informed Norm that there was a message for him to carry to the next car, he set his glove and ball on the seat and jumped to his feet. He walked proudly to the back of the car, where he was handed a folded piece of paper with a name written on it. The MP opened the door, keeping a close eye on him. For a moment he was outside on the connecting walkway between the two train cars. He experienced a rush of cool air, which felt great after the stuffy car, and he saw a glimpse of open country before the MP in the next car opened the door and took the note from him.

It all happened so quickly that Norm wondered why they even bothered with messengers. In another minute he was back in his seat. He had thought this adventure would be more like riding for the Pony Express, only without a horse. Instead, it had been almost nothing. Later he delivered another message, this time getting to walk through two cars, and that was the last one for the trip.

That night he tried to sleep, but it was hard to do sitting up and there was no way to lie down. Only small children and babies seemed to be actually sleeping. When morning finally came, he felt grumpy and groggy. Children were crying and everyone was hungry. Norm wished for scrambled eggs or oatmeal. He would have settled for any-thing, but the snacks were all gone.

It was almost 9 a.m. when the train started to slow. The 350-mile trip had taken sixteen hours. Norm wanted to cheer because it was finally over, but he knew to sit quietly in his seat. The MPs came along the aisle announcing that they would arrive at Santa Anita in a few minutes and they could raise the shades when the train stopped. So the famed racetrack was indeed their destination!

As Norm heard the hiss of the brakes and felt the final jolt of the train, shades went up all around him and daylight filled the car. Papa leaned over to look out the window with Norm. The train tracks went right up to the gate at Santa Anita, and the first thing they saw was barbed wire. Behind it, men, women—and children—peered out at the train. Papa put a reassuring hand on Norm's shoulder. Norm remembered a newspaper photo of prisoners of war behind barbed wire somewhere in Europe. But this was America.

Long considered one of the world's most beautiful racetracks, this panoramic view shows what Santa Anita looked like with 500 barracks filling its vast parking lots.

The presence of so many soldiers alarmed evacuees arriving at Santa Anita. They now realized beyond a doubt that they were prisoners.

He couldn't remember ever seeing a photo showing American prisoners who were children. And he was now one of them.

With the MPs shouting instructions, everyone lined up to file off the train. Norm held his ball and glove tightly. As he stepped onto sturdy ground at last, he stretched in the sunshine, grateful to be outside and free of the train's confinement. He stayed close to his family as they searched through the luggage being unloaded on the train platform to find their own. MPs checked that luggage tags matched the family's assigned number.

Norm tried not to stare at the watchtowers visible every few hundred feet along the barbed wire fence. He felt a stab of alarm when he realized that the guards in the towers were armed with rifles and machine guns.

MPs marched everyone into the camp. Norm looked around. Crowds of men, women, and children were everywhere. He had never seen so many people all in one place. With the arrival of the last evacuees from San Jose and Los Angeles, nineteen thousand people were now imprisoned at Santa Anita, making it the largest of the fifteen assembly centers.

Once again they waited, this time standing in a long line while their paperwork was processed. Norm kept looking around for Eddie, hoping he'd come to see the train arrive, but it was hard to spot anyone in the dense crowd and in all the confusion. Norm was both curious and anxious about where they would be living.

Military police in towers like this one atop the Santa Anita stadium monitored inmates around the clock.

Upon arrival, internees faced several tasks, including finding their luggage and filling out more paperwork.

His stomach rumbled. *Please let breakfast be next!* Instead, MPs walked their group of new arrivals to an open area where Norm saw a mountain of straw. At first he didn't understand when an officer in charge told them they were to make mattresses. At home he slept on a comfortable, well-constructed mattress. Surely they weren't going to sleep on straw! But they were given large bags made of rough cotton ticking and were told to stuff them with the straw because yes, these would be their mattresses.

Norm could feel his family's astonishment, though no one said anything. They set down their suitcases and got to work. The straw was dusty and scratchy and Norm's Cub Scout uniform was getting dirty. He didn't like the way the straw smelled. His family had on their best clothes, and here they were, stuffing rough bags with straw. Helen said softly that they were lucky none of them had hay fever, or they would really suffer.

It pained Norm to see his mother and sisters doing this demeaning task, and he knew it must be terrible for Papa and Albert to not be allowed to do it for them. Papa urged Norm to stuff his bag as full as he could to eliminate lumps. "You're going to have to sleep on this and you want to be as comfortable as possible," he said.

The work was hard and the day had gotten warm. When everyone finished, a flatbed army truck pulled into the area and MPs instructed them to get aboard. Norm struggled to carry his glove and ball, his suitcases, and the large, awkward mattress. Albert hopped up on the truck so he could hoist up mattresses and suitcases and help people climb aboard.

New arrivals at Santa Anita, like these at Poston War Relocation Center in Arizona, were dismayed at having to stuff their own mattresses.

As the truck pulled into a massive parking lot, Norm saw endless rows of newly built wooden barracks, lined up as far as the eye could see. They looked like large shacks covered in black tar paper. There were five hundred of them, each with six rooms all in a row. Each room had a window and a door to the outside. Norm knew this was where they would be living. He tried not to think about their comfortable home back in San Jose. What had they done to deserve this?

His mother gasped when she saw the twenty-by-twenty-foot room assigned to their family. Six metal army cots, each with two blankets, were the only furnishings. No chairs, no table, no carpet, no running water. No bathroom, kitchen, or closet. A lone lightbulb hung from the ceiling. There was one electrical outlet. Through the thin walls

Living conditions at Santa Anita were primitive. Initially it had only 150 showers for 19,000 inmates.

they could hear every noise and every word being said in the rooms on either side of them. Six people in one small space, no privacy to change clothes, no water for washing, no curtain on the window.

Norm kept quiet. He'd only have to stay in this room to sleep.

Mama seemed to be in a daze. Etsu and Helen were, too. Trying to sound cheerful, Papa suggested they all go use the restrooms and then come back to get organized. Lunch would be soon, he assured them. Norm hoped he was right.

The men's communal bathroom was another shock. They had to wait in a long line to get in. Once inside, they found a large open room with no privacy for either showers or toilets. If the women's restroom was as open as the men's, Norm knew his mother and sisters would feel embarrassed to be so exposed.

There wasn't a single bathtub. Norm was used to baths, but showers were okay, too. However, older Japanese like Mama and Papa considered baths a sacred daily ritual—San Jose's Japantown even had a bathhouse—and Norm wondered how his parents would adjust.

When they had all returned to the room, no one said anything about the bathrooms, but Mama, Etsu, and Helen were visibly upset.

A moment later they heard the ringing of a bell. Finally, lunchtime! They followed others from their barracks to the mess hall. Norm was so hungry he thought he could eat cardboard. People ate in thirty-minute shifts, and the Minetas had to stand in line for an hour to get in. First they went through the food line to get served, then sat on benches at tables to eat. When they finished they scraped and stacked their dishes and then took them to the kitchen. Norm noticed that some people brought their own chopsticks, but Papa and Mama both said that they would make do with the camp silverware.

Lunch was a boiled potato, a slice of Spam, a piece of bread, and a

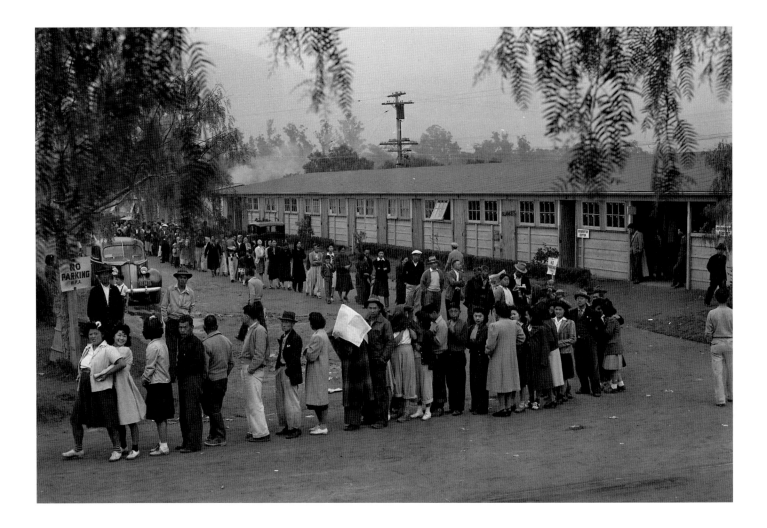

Internees at Santa Anita typically waited in line for meals for over an hour. Once inside, a shortage of seating meant people had to eat quickly.

serving of canned fruit. Though Norm liked Spam, his sisters didn't, so Mama rarely served it at home. But it was this or nothing. They ate without complaining.

A man sitting next to Albert told them the food was better than when he first arrived a month ago, even though most of it came from cans. A woman across the table suggested they buy soy sauce at the camp store and bring it with them to meals because the cooks didn't use spices and everything tasted the same.

Norm knew his parents would be glad to hear about the soy sauce. He was just happy the mess hall had ketchup, which he loved.

After lunch the family returned to the room to finish unpacking and organizing. Then they took a walk around Santa Anita, hoping they would run into people from home. Before the afternoon was over, they'd not only connected with friends, but one of them said the Kimura family was there and even knew where they lived. Papa went with Norm to find them. When Eddie came to the door and saw Norm, the two boys just grinned at each other. Very quickly they were racing around excitedly in front of the barracks. Eddie's brother John joined them. They told Norm that their friends Richard and Tom had been sent to a different assembly center.

Papa wanted to visit with the Kimuras, and Eddie and John wanted to show Norm the camp. "Be sure you know how to get back to our barracks. Come in time for us to go to supper together," Papa told Norm.

The boys sped off. Eddie and John had already figured out Santa Anita's layout and were eager for Norm to see it all. They showed him the post office. Norm was glad to know its location because he knew his parents would be posting a letter immediately to Aya to let her know where they were. Then they went into the camp store to look around. Anything from snacks to clothing could be purchased there, and Norm was pleased to see that it had a freezer with ice-cream bars and Popsicles—but he was disappointed that they didn't carry his favorite: Creamsicles, with vanilla ice cream covered in orange-flavored ice.

They saw the administrative offices and then the flagpole where the American flag was raised each morning. Norm asked if any horses were still at Santa Anita. Eddie said he'd heard that there had been a thousand Thoroughbreds there, but they had all been taken somewhere else. Even with no horses, Norm was impressed with everything he saw.

In the racetrack infield, people tended a large garden filled with vegetable plants. The huge grandstand, which could seat twenty-six thousand people, was filled with activity. In one area young people had a record player and couples were dancing to the music. In other parts of the stadium, people were involved in various classes. A group of women were knitting, and in a far corner, a choir was rehearsing.

Internees hired to construct camouflage nets enjoyed working outside, but the job was tedious and tiresome.

"We have Sunday church services over there," Eddie said, pointing to another area of the massive stadium.

Norm saw young men and women constructing gigantic camouflage nets that would be used to cover military property so it couldn't be seen from above if there was an enemy air strike. "They get paid to do that," John said. "So do people who work in the cafeteria or help clean the bathrooms."

"But they only get paid a little, and not everyone who wants a job can find one," Eddie said.

Norm noticed that most of the adults looked gloomy, while younger people and all the kids seemed to be having a good time. One large group was practicing for a talent show that would be held Saturday evening. "We get to see movies every Friday night," Eddie said. "And we don't have to go to school! Mostly we just play softball and baseball. We have lots of teams here."

Soon Norm was involved in a pickup baseball game. He told the boys his bat had been taken away from him and they nodded. "We aren't allowed to have our own, but they have bats here that we can use."

When Norm learned that families were living in horse stalls in the stables, he was jealous. Maybe his family could have lived in Seabiscuit's stall if they'd arrived at Santa Anita earlier. But Eddie said, "You might not like it. Our friends will show you theirs."

After the visit Norm knew his family was lucky to be in the barracks. The partitions between stalls didn't reach all the way to the ceiling, and the stables were very noisy. Stall spaces were so tiny that occupants had to climb over one metal cot to get to the next. And that wasn't the worst part: Norm had noticed a faint smell of horse manure. "Do they all smell like that, or just the one we saw?" he asked.

Eddie held his nose. "They're all that way. Everyone cleans and scrubs and they still smell."

That night after the mandatory lights-out at 10 p.m., Norm lay awake on his scratchy, rough mattress. The straw had a dank smell, but now he knew he could be smelling something a lot worse. As tired as he was, every time he started to drift off to sleep the searchlight from the closest guard tower flashed across the bare window, back and forth, back and forth. He covered his head with his blanket, but he could still see the light, and he would see it ever after in his dreams.

He thought about everything that had happened that day. He could hardly believe that he and his family were there, crowded together in one room.

Hard as he tried, he couldn't get the guard towers out of his mind. "When I first looked up at them, I remembered how the government had been telling us that the camps were for our protection. But if that was true, why were the guards' guns pointed at us?"

CHAPTER 8

Into the Wilderness

Until it happened, Norm could not have guessed how challenging it would be for his family to live in confinement. He and Albert had shared a room just a little smaller than this at home, but now Etsu, Helen, and Mama and Papa were right there, too. They hung a blanket in a corner to create a tiny space where one person could dress with a little privacy. They made the room as tidy as possible, and Mama kept every surface spotless. They were out of the room much of the day, since hours were spent standing in lines: lines to use the bathrooms, lines to get into the mess hall to eat, and lines to send letters and get their mail.

Both Papa and Mama visited daily with San Jose friends in the camp, and they wrote weekly to Aya. Because of Papa's reputation back home, he quickly became a leader at Santa Anita. He was sought out to discuss news of the war and what was happening in the camp. He always counseled optimism and cooperation, assuring others that better days were ahead.

Mama concentrated on housekeeping. At home she had a washing machine. But here, every item of clothing, every towel and sheet had to be washed by hand. Norm helped her carry laundry to the communal laundry facility, where they waited for a turn to scrub sheets and clothes on washboards in one of the few sinks. Then Norm helped carry everything back to the room. Papa had strung a clothesline from one corner to the other, and they hung all the wet items on it. Mama had always taken great pride in caring for her family and home. She was still upset that she was not allowed to have an iron.

The women stayed busy with children and housework, but men had little to do. For them, boredom was a big problem. Mostly they sat around talking with each other. "Japanese Americans have a strong work ethic, but there were very few jobs," Norm said. "Being outside helped. The weather was perfect. The landscape was beautiful, and in the distance we could see the San Gabriel Mountains."

Norm's brother and sisters managed to get paying work. Albert was hired to help make the camouflage netting for the military. Both Helen and Etsu found jobs in the camp administration as secretaries. Albert was paid $12 a month, and Etsu and Helen were each paid $16. It wasn't much, but it helped buy items at the camp store like the soy sauce Mama and Papa now brought with them to meals, and other things they always needed, including shampoo, toothpaste, and laundry detergent.

"We bought only necessities. We didn't know how long our money had to last," Norm said. "It felt like the war could go on forever. We were fighting Japan in the Pacific, and Hitler and the Italian dictator Mussolini in Europe. Besides, we knew we'd soon be sent to a permanent camp and we'd have to leave behind anything we couldn't carry."

Norm found plenty to do every day. He met up with Eddie and John right after breakfast and they spent their time inventing games, exploring the camp, and playing baseball and marbles.

Sometimes they watched the older kids dancing to records in the grandstand. A dance was held every Saturday night with live music. Although Mama opposed dancing, she enjoyed good music, and the Minetas and Kimuras often came to listen to the camp musicians playing the big band sound of Glenn Miller and the popular hits of Bing Crosby, the Andrews Sisters, and Frank Sinatra.

As Papa observed all the young people dancing, he commented that some of them were probably doing it over the objections of their traditional parents. He predicted trouble for these families. He knew from discussions with concerned parents that they felt they were losing control of their older children, who were staying out late, spending all their time with friends, and even eating meals with them. The camp atmosphere gave young people freedom they'd never known before, and some were rebelling.

"Papa insisted that we have breakfast and dinner together as a family," Norm said. " 'Do what you want during the day,' he told us, 'but for these two meals, we will walk to the mess hall together and sit down and eat together.' My brother and sisters and I never questioned this because having meals together as a family was as strong a tradition in Japanese culture as obeying the father. Eddie's family was the same."

For adults, the crowded bathrooms and lack of privacy were daily issues. Mama, especially, suffered humiliation by having to shower in the open, but nothing could be done about it. She and Etsu and Helen tried to take showers at odd times when the bathrooms weren't so crowded. If it was already dark, the searchlight from the guard tower followed them to and from the bathroom to show them the way, but this caused even more embarrassment.

For Norm, showers were fun. He and his friends often went to the horse paddocks to take them where the horses had formerly been washed down. The shower rooms were large and round, and shower heads lined the walls. The boys happily stood in the open, water spraying them from all sides as they joked about showering with Seabiscuit. "We loved it," Norm said.

In midsummer Helen left the camp. Internees could be released if they secured approved jobs that helped ease labor shortages in places other than the restricted area along the West Coast. Good secretaries were in short supply during the war, for women workers were badly needed in factories to take over work formerly done by men now in the military—and factory jobs paid far better than secretarial work. Helen's boss at San Jose State told a friend in Chicago about her, and as a result Helen was offered the position of executive secretary to the president of a Chicago corporation. Santa Anita administrators approved the job, and in July Helen moved. She found a room to rent in a private home in Evanston, Illinois, a suburb of Chicago, and began working in the city, where she did not know a single person. Norm hated to see her go, but at least she would no longer be living behind barbed wire.

Shortly after she departed, he received a package from her with a copy of the book *Gulliver's Travels*. "She worried that I was not in school and thought it would be good for me to spend time reading," he said. "I was not happy since reading was so hard for me. But Mama insisted that I do it and also answer a list of questions Helen sent about the book. It was tough having a sister whose true ambition was to be a teacher."

Norm was sure Etsu would also leave soon—for Salt Lake City. She and Mike were engaged, and camp policy would allow her to leave if she was getting married, as long as she did not return to the restricted area.

One day in early August there was a near riot at Santa Anita. People had gathered to protest the low wages paid for camp jobs, as well as military searches of personal belongings. Some people had things stolen from them during these searches. To prevent an actual riot, military police shot their weapons into the air. People panicked and fled. Norm, Eddie, and John were playing nearby when they heard gunfire. "We dropped to the ground, scared to death. When we didn't hear any more shots, we got out of there fast," Norm said. "I was really shook. It was another reminder that we were prisoners and things could go wrong if we dared question anything."

By September, internees were beginning to be moved to the permanent camps. They now knew that there were ten of them: two in California, two in Arizona, two in Arkansas, and one each in Colorado, Utah, Wyoming, and Idaho. Aya and Min and his relatives were sent to the Central Utah War Relocation Center, which was known as Topaz. Aya wrote that the internment camp was named for Topaz Mountain. Even in early autumn, she said, the weather was very cold and was a shock for all of them.

Norm knew his family's turn would come soon. In November, just a couple of weeks after Norm's eleventh birthday, the Minetas learned they were leaving. They had been at Santa Anita almost six months. Most internees boarded trains not knowing where they were being sent. But somehow Papa learned the day before they departed that they were going to Wyoming. The Kimuras had left a couple of days earlier, and Norm hoped with all his might that Eddie was also headed there.

Once again he had a number pinned to his clothing and his luggage. The train he and his parents, Etsu, and Albert were on chugged along on tracks headed northeast, away from Southern California and its perpetual blue skies. Just as before, window shades had to be down. This time Norm wasn't allowed to be a messenger, and Helen wasn't with them. The trip would take four days and three nights.

They had been told food would be provided, so they brought no snacks. They quickly regretted this: by the second day they were tired of the sandwiches they were given for every meal.

On the third day, the MPs announced a brief stop in Salt Lake City to switch crews. Etsu couldn't believe they were stopping in the city she hoped to soon move to, but the worst part was that she knew Mike was traveling for his job, so even if she had been allowed to see him, she wouldn't have been able to. Also, Topaz, where Aya and Min were, was just 140 miles from Salt Lake City. But they were prisoners and so were Norm and his family, so there would be no possibility of seeing each other.

Internees at Santa Anita prepare to board trains to permanent camps.

"We were told we could get off the train when it stopped, but we quickly found out that we were inside a service area that was sealed off from the rest of the train station," Norm said. "The only place to stand was on the platform alongside the train. The November air was about forty degrees out, which felt very cold to us. None of us had any warm clothing."

To everyone's surprise, a young Japanese American woman came into the area and approached one of the MPs. "She said she lived in Salt Lake City. Somehow she had learned that her father was on our train," Norm said. "She didn't try to find him, she just handed a box of cigars to the MP and asked him to give it to her father, who loved cigars.

"The MP opened the box in front of her and crumbled the cigars into tiny pieces. Then he dropped the box on the ground. Many people witnessed her humiliation. For her to be treated so disrespectfully showed us yet again what was thought of us."

The journey resumed. Outside the air grew colder and colder. Late in the afternoon of the fourth day, the train came to a final stop and the shades went up. Norm looked out at a muted brown landscape. Sagebrush and dust whipped along through the bleakness. He did not see a single tree. Behind the barbed wire fence he could see tar paper–covered barracks. Later he would notice the sign that said HEART MOUNTAIN WAR RELOCATION CENTER.

As he climbed down from the train, the freezing wind took his breath away. "We were dressed for California," he said. "I had no coat, just a light jacket. The cold pierced my skin. I heard a guard say that the wind chill was well below zero. We got our luggage and climbed aboard trucks where we sat on open benches in the wind.

"Inside the camp we were greeted with the same armed guards and guard towers that were at Santa Anita. After four days on the train, we were filthy and also exhausted from trying to sleep sitting up. Thankfully we weren't hungry. We'd had sandwiches on the train a short while earlier."

By the time they were processed into the camp and taken to their assigned barracks, it was dark outside. Once again "home" was a small room furnished only with metal cots. At least this time they had real mattresses. As before, a bare lightbulb hung from the ceiling. The tar paper was the only insulation, and frigid air came through the walls and small window. Norm was so cold that he wondered if he would freeze to death.

But Papa was already at work getting a fire started in the small coal-burning potbellied stove that sat in the corner. Norm stretched out on one of the cots. The room gradually warmed, and he was soon asleep.

CHAPTER 9

Heart Mountain

The family awoke the next morning to a cold room and the mournful sound of the Wyoming wind beating against the outside walls. Since the barracks were constructed up off the ground, the wind swirled underneath them, coming up through cracks in the floor. Papa restarted the fire. Mama found a piece of cardboard, and she and Etsu used it to try to sweep up the dust that had seeped in overnight. It was everywhere. Norm could even taste it in his mouth.

He needed to go to the bathroom. He needed a shower. And he was very hungry. Papa said showers would have to wait until after breakfast because they had to get to the mess hall at their assigned time. They all dressed quickly and hurried off to the communal bathrooms, a half block from the barracks, trying not to slip on the fresh snow that had fallen overnight, coating the uneven ground. The freezing wind cut Norm's skin as he stood in line with Papa and Albert. He had layered several shirts under his lightweight jacket, but he had no gloves, hat, heavy coat, warm socks, or winter boots. "We'll order everything we need today," Papa told him. "Someone will lend us their catalog."

Some internees filled the space under their barracks with dirt in an attempt to control the cold and dust that came up through the floorboards. Others kept the space open and used it to store items like sleds and work tools.

Norm brightened at the thought of picking out things from the catalog. At Santa Anita the mail-order catalogs from Montgomery Ward and Sears Roebuck had been prized items. They carried just about anything anyone could want. He had loved looking through them, imagining all the things he would buy if only there were enough money and extra storage space. But now, warm clothes were a necessity and space would have to be found. The hard part would be mailing off the order and having to wait the two weeks it typically took for a catalog order to arrive.

The mess hall they entered for breakfast was just like Santa Anita's, located in a barracks with the kitchen and serving counter on one side looking out at a room filled with tables and benches. Going through the line, Norm had a choice of either scrambled eggs and toast, or toast and a single-serving box of cereal. He chose Wheaties, the "Breakfast of Champions," thinking it might give him the boost he needed that day.

While they ate, Papa visited with the man seated next to him. When the man got up to leave, he handed Papa the latest issue of the *Heart Mountain Sentinel*. This was the camp newspaper that was printed every Saturday at the newspaper office in the nearby town of Cody. They printed 5,000 copies and some of it was in Japanese for those internees who couldn't read English.

Heart Mountain's mess hall was just like Santa Anita's, with food served cafeteria style.

Papa looked through it and then handed it to Norm, who was surprised at how professional it looked. He later found out that the Heart Mountain newspaper was considered by many to be the best written and edited of all the camps' newspapers. "It was full of camp news," Norm said. "We looked forward to it every week and read every word. It helped us to feel less isolated from the rest of the world since it also reported news about the war."

When the family finished eating, they scraped and stacked their dishes and returned them to the kitchen. Norm had already memorized their camp address: Block 24, Barracks 7, Unit B. On their way back, Papa stopped for a moment, pointing at the mountain in the distance. It was barely visible through overcast skies. Heart Mountain War Relocation Center—simply called Heart Mountain by everyone—was named for it. Norm studied it. The odd, boxy shape didn't look like a heart at all. And it wasn't nearly as majestic and beautiful as mountains he'd seen in California's Yosemite National Park.

As Norm looked around at the dull, gray landscape, he felt a stab of longing for California and its warm sun, green grass, and bright flowers. How would they survive here? He was so cold that his teeth chattered and his feet were numb. He wondered how he would find Eddie in this huge camp, assuming Eddie was even here. Maybe he would find him at school.

Heart Mountain had two elementary schools set up in empty barracks. Norm's class had forty students—many more than his school in San Jose—but to Norm's dismay, Eddie wasn't one of them. Norm sat with other students on long benches, and they shared the few

On freezing winter days, guards manning the towers also suffered from the cold.

textbooks available while they waited for the arrival of new ones. In other parts of the camp, students sat on stools and used orange crates for desks. Internees with carpentry skills were busy building student desks and chairs in the camp woodworking shop.

Teachers were in short supply since so many were now in the military or working in the defense industry. Norm's teacher was Dorothea Foucar, a Quaker from Denver who had come to teach at the camp. Like other Quakers, she believed that the internment of Japanese Americans was not only morally wrong, but a violation of their constitutional rights.

Norm knew right away how fortunate he was, for his new teacher

Internees with carpentry skills helped build chairs and desks for the schools.

Norm's teacher, Mrs. Foucar, is fifth from the left in the back row in this picture of her with other Heart Mountain educators.

was an excellent instructor who cared deeply about each student. "She wanted to know if you were okay," Norm said. "Not just were you learning, but was your life okay. Mrs. Foucar wouldn't have known about dyslexia back then, but she saw that I had a problem and spent a great deal of time figuring out learning strategies to help me. Reading and math became easier, and I looked forward to school every day."

Although most teachers were white, a few were Japanese Americans interned at Heart Mountain. Norm and many of his classmates had been out of school for at least six months, and to get them caught up, both teachers and students worked very hard.

Education in the camp was overseen by the state of Wyoming, and a brick high school building was under construction and would offer the same facilities as other Wyoming high schools. But plans to build new elementary schools were scrapped when upset Wyoming citizens complained that the internees were, after all, prisoners of war, and that they were being treated too well.

It took Norm a week to find Eddie. Once again the boys had a happy reunion. But this time they faced several major obstacles to playing together.

The first was the size of the camp. Santa Anita had comprised a few hundred acres, but Heart Mountain was huge: twenty thousand acres in all. The government owned all the land and had enclosed just under 750 acres with barbed wire to create the camp, which had nine guard towers around the perimeter. It housed more than ten thousand internees in 467 barracks that were organized into twenty different blocks, each with about five hundred people. Every block had its own mess hall, communal bathrooms, and laundry.

There was also a group of buildings set apart from the main camp that housed apartments for teachers, military police, and administrative staff who didn't stay in nearby towns. Additionally, there were administrative offices for the 130 staff members who oversaw the day-to-day operations of the camp, and buildings that housed the hospital, the camp store, the post office, and churches.

Eddie's barracks was a thirty-minute walk from Norm's, and that distance became especially difficult in the winter months. "It was dark by four thirty in the afternoon," Norm said. "The camp had no paved sidewalks or streets. No streetlights, either. Just those high-beam spotlights from the guard towers. Without them, you could easily stumble and fall. Lots of people were injured that way."

And with so many barracks that looked exactly alike, getting lost

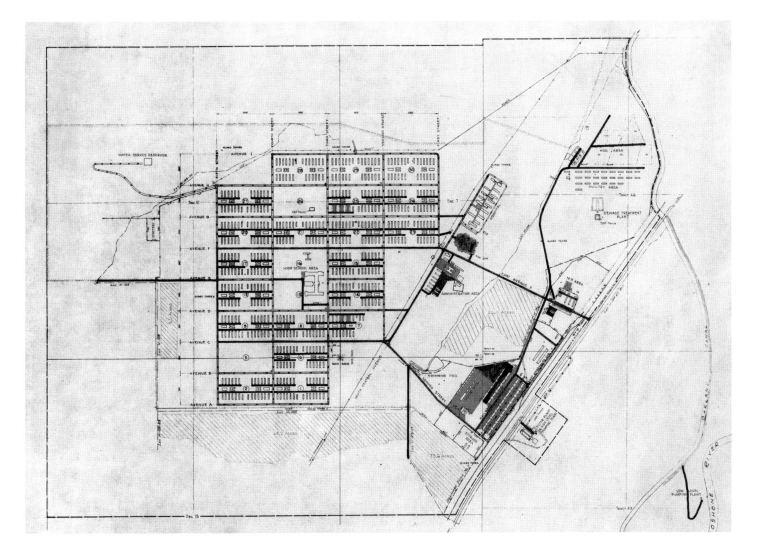

was another obstacle. In daylight the position of the mountain helped with direction, but nothing helped at night.

"We still saw each other, just not very much," Norm said. "The Kimuras went to a different mess hall, and Eddie and I both ate our meals with our parents. His school was far from mine. We both had chores. I had homework every day, plus Helen was still sending me books—*Robinson Crusoe* arrived, and then *The Adventures of Tom Sawyer*—and my mother expected me to read them. It was too hard after dark with only a single lightbulb in our room, so I had to do it after school."

The fenced portion of Heart Mountain measured a mile and a half from one corner diagonally to the other, and it took about an hour to walk across the rough ground.

But on weekends, when Norm had some free time, outside was the place to be, no matter how bad the weather. It was always very cold, and many nights it snowed, but once he bundled up in his new winter gear from the catalog, he was okay. He discovered that the camp had several ice-skating rinks, one right by his barracks. His parents ordered skates for him, and ice skating became his favorite winter pastime. Sometimes Eddie and John came over to skate. Otherwise, Norm was with boys who lived close by. "Most were from Los Angeles," Norm said. "I made several new friends."

The best thing about all the snow was snowball fights. They were a daily occurrence. Sledding would have been more popular if there

Internees embraced ice skating and sledding—activities that allowed them to enjoy the cold, get exercise, and socialize.

had been places to store sleds. A few parents ordered them from the catalog and figured out somewhere to keep them—usually under the barracks—but Mama and Papa said no. Instead, Norm and Eddie used big cardboard boxes that they flattened.

One memorable day when the snow was tightly packed and glazed with ice crystals, they started at the top of a long, gentle slope that ended at the barbed wire fence. They'd never had trouble stopping at the bottom. But this time the slope was so slick that they found themselves racing toward the fence with no way to stop. "I pressed my head as flat as I could against the cardboard, scared that I was going to get caught on those sharp barbs," Norm said. "The ground must have dipped a bit right there, because both Eddie and I slid right under the fence wire and were suddenly outside camp proper."

Just then an MP patrol jeep pulled up beside them. "Halt!" shouted the guards. "We were so scared," Norm said. "Eddie thought they might shoot us. All I worried about was that they'd notify my dad." The guards ordered the boys into the back of the jeep and drove them inside the camp to the administration building. Then Norm's father was summoned.

"Papa was pretty upset with me," Norm said. "In Japanese culture a father is dishonored if he cannot control his own child. He probably knew I wasn't being disobedient, but I had caused him embarrassment. Eddie and I still went sledding after that, but we were very careful."

CHAPTER 10

New Routines

Every day of the week, Norm had chores. Each morning he helped shake out bedding to get rid of all the dust that had sifted into the room overnight. He also checked everybody's shoes to make sure no spiders had crawled into them, for some Wyoming spiders were active in winter. At least black widow spiders—and rattlesnakes, too—were dormant when the weather was very cold. Norm had heard that both were sighted frequently in and around the camp in warm weather.

His most important chore was to gather coal for their stove. Coal arrived daily by train and a huge pile was dumped outside each of the communal bathrooms. To provide a day's worth of fuel, Norm had to make three or four trips to the pile, sort through the pieces to find the best ones, and then carry them in a metal bucket to the room. When he was done, he made the trek back to the restroom to scrub the black dust off his hands. He tried hard to keep it off his clothes so he wouldn't make extra work for his mother when she washed them.

On Saturdays he helped Mama with the wash just as he had at

In the coldest weather, the train bringing coal sometimes arrived late. The moment the coal was dumped into a pile, people rushed to get some for their potbellied stoves.

Santa Anita. The two of them carried clothes, sheets, and towels to the laundry room in a big basket and waited in line for one of the large sinks. Mama scrubbed each item on a washboard, and Norm rinsed it and wrung out as much water as possible. Then they carried the wet items back to the barracks in the basket and hung everything on the clothesline that Papa had put up.

Norm felt sorry for young mothers who had to wash stacks of cloth diapers, which, like all clothing, froze solid on the trip back to the barracks. With no bathtubs for bathing small children, many mothers washed them, as well as their family's clothing, sheets, and towels, in the deep laundry-room sinks. This was no easy task. Children had to be bundled up for the walk from the barracks to the washroom, then unbundled and bathed, and then bundled up again. Some families purchased little red wagons from a catalog to haul everything—including small children—to and from the laundry.

Internee Estelle Peck Ishigo drew many pictures of daily life at Heart Mountain, including this one of a laundry room and the ones on pages 91 and 93.

Pulling a wagon over the rough frozen ground was hazardous, but if it tipped over, someone was always nearby to help.

The laundry room was a congenial place where women could visit and gossip. Norm liked listening in. But the older women, including his mother, usually conversed in Japanese. "I wanted to know what they were saying, so I was motivated to try to figure out the words I didn't understand. It improved my Japanese," Norm said.

The laundry rooms also had sewing machines—and irons, which pleased Mama—and they were in use all the time. "All of us did everything we could to keep neat and clean. We considered it a source of pride to always look our best," Norm said. "It was not only a part of our culture—it also kept us from giving in to despair. Rips and tears were carefully mended by hand or on the machines. Mama and Etsu bought inexpensive fabric and dress patterns at the camp store and sewed up the latest fashions. To complete the look, they always wore their hair in the newest styles."

Everyone welcomed getting out of the barracks for any reason, but the bitter cold weather made it difficult. Frostbite was a real danger. "We learned later that the winter of 1942–43 was the coldest on record in Wyoming, with heavy snows, ice, and windstorms," Norm said. "Every night temperatures plunged below freezing. It was very challenging for all of us.

"So was using the restrooms. You could be anywhere from a

Many women considered the lack of privacy in the bathrooms to be the hardest thing they endured. Younger women adapted more easily than older ones.

few yards to hundreds of yards away from them. To get to them in darkness or semidarkness, it was easy to stumble on the rough, uneven ground. If the line to get in was long, you could turn numb waiting in the cold."

Several times a week after school Norm went to the camp post office to stand in a long line in the icy cold to mail letters and pick up incoming mail. An average of 3,500 pieces of mail left Heart Mountain every day. Almost as many came in. The family eagerly awaited letters from Helen, who was enjoying her job in Chicago, and from Aya in Utah.

"From what Aya wrote, their camp was like ours, though a little smaller," Norm said. "She said that the air was very dusty and extremely cold and that she and Min were fortunate that their barracks was close to both the mess hall and bathrooms. We couldn't get past the irony that Aya and Min were in an internment camp in Utah, and that Mike lived in the same state but was free."

Papa and Mama did what they could to make their barracks room as comfortable as possible. They hung a blanket to create a private dressing space in one corner. When long-delayed sheets of wall insulation arrived at the camp, Papa and Albert hauled it to the room and covered the walls, cutting and fitting it carefully to eliminate all gaps.

"What a difference the insulation made!" said Norm. "It cut down on the dust and we were much warmer. It also helped reduce noise from other rooms in the barracks."

Over time, Mama sewed many things, including curtains for the window. Papa enjoyed woodworking—he'd had a workshop back home in San Jose—and at the camp's shop he built a coal box, a dresser, and a table for the room from scrap lumber. He also built a toolbox and ordered basic tools from the catalog. He patched the room's floor, making it airtight so dust couldn't get in.

Soon Papa had a job, one reserved for Issei only. "My father be-

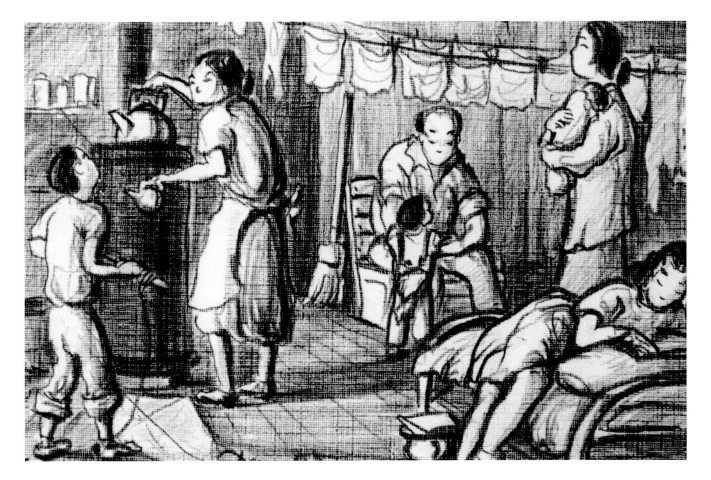

came our block chairman," Norm said. "He was like the mayor. He was our representative to the camp administration. We also had a block manager, who was a Nisei, and his job was to make sure we followed camp policies. We all knew the administration decided everything, but at least we felt like we had a voice."

In spite of noise, crowding, no water, and only one light-bulb and one electrical outlet, internees managed to make their cramped rooms livable.

Albert had brought along his college textbooks and studied all the time. He was hoping he could return to college with the help of the Quakers, who worked to find colleges and universities willing to accept students from the camps. The government allowed internees to leave, provided the school was outside the restricted area.

Since the camp administration always needed secretaries, Etsu was quickly hired at a salary of $14 a month. She was employed when the new camp director, Guy Robertson, took over in December.

Compared to administrators in some of the other camps, he was progressive in his thinking. It wasn't realistic that thousands of people imprisoned against their will at Heart Mountain could be a close-knit community, but he hoped to make their experience more endurable. "He would listen to reason," Norm said.

As Christmas approached, holiday music filled the camp. Norm loved singing along to popular Christmas songs like "Jingle Bells" and "'Twas the Night Before Christmas." In spite of the bitter weather, lots of groups formed to go caroling. Some of them would trudge all the way to the hospital out on the edge of camp to sing to patients.

One night on a whim a group of Heart Mountain carolers stopped at the base of one of the guard towers and sang. A caroler later recalled that once they were done, "We heard this poor voice, almost choking with tears, saying 'Thank you!' How lonely he must have been up there."

Some internees ordered small gifts from the catalogs or found something at the camp store, but most were too concerned about money. "We agreed that there would be no gifts," Norm said. "We got our rent check for our house in San Jose every month, so we were fortunate, but we were still very careful about what we spent. Papa made $16 a month working as our block chairman, and the government provided our food, housing, and medical care, but we still had other expenses."

Had the Minetas been at home in San Jose they would have decorated a tall, fresh tree in the living room and gone to Christmas Eve services at their church, where Norm would have participated in the Sunday-school Christmas pageant. On Christmas morning they would have opened their gifts and then joined Eddie's family and other friends for a huge dinner.

At Heart Mountain, the only event to attend was a nondenominational church service. "We wished each other a Merry Christmas, even though it wasn't so merry. And we had no Christmas tree and no special meal," Norm said. "Most of all, we missed Aya and Helen and spoke with longing about the day when we could all be together again."

Living primitively in close confinement with little control of their own future created considerable stress for everyone. Norm did not feel it like some people, because his parents stayed positive. Remarkably, so did many other internees. Upsets and arguments occurred, and a few people gave in to despair so deep that they never recovered. Yet the majority subscribed to a philosophy Norm understood as samurai fortitude: the ability to endure.

"The philosophy of Zen means, simply, if you can't change it, you accept it and make the best of it—a way of living passed down to us from our ancestors," Norm said. "And that's what we did."

CHAPTER 11

Making the Best of It

It wasn't just the wind that sometimes woke Norm in the night. It was also the mournful howls of wolves and coyotes out beyond the perimeter of the camp. When he heard these sounds, he was grateful that his family was close around him, and he usually fell back to sleep quickly.

The feelings he had about the mountain his first day at the camp had started to change. Heart Mountain rose from the valley of the Big Horn Basin to an elevation of just over eight thousand feet, and at certain times of day the camp was in its shadow. "It was the focal point of the landscape, always there, ever changing, depending on the light. But whether we could even see it depended on the clouds, fog, sleet, or snow," Norm said.

"We weren't sure who named it. One story we heard was that it was sacred to the area's Native Americans and that the Crow Nation called it Heart Mountain because its shape resembled a buffalo heart. I grew to believe it was watching over us and to love it. I never tired of looking at it. I could draw its shape with my eyes closed."

Severe weather made January and February of 1943 especially difficult at Heart Mountain. They were also difficult months across America. The war effort required so much in the way of materials and supplies that food was rationed—sugar, meat, coffee, butter, and much more—and so were many everyday items like gasoline, tires, shoes, and women's nylon stockings. The military was experiencing high casualties in both Europe and the Pacific, and the war had no end in sight. In the internment camps, Norm and everyone else wondered if they would ever be able to go back to their homes.

Fortunately, the government was now allowing even more internees to leave the camps to help fill labor shortages. Some hired out as day laborers in areas surrounding their camps. Some moved to other states, as long as work sites weren't in the restricted area on the west coast. Most jobs were on farms and in factories. Internees at Heart Mountain helped local farmers harvest and process sugar beets and soybeans, the area's two biggest crops. A few found jobs helping with housework or child care for people in Cody and Powell, taking the local bus to work in the towns.

In spite of the country's deep-seated prejudice against anyone with Japanese ancestry, Papa's loyalty to the United States was unwavering. Although he wasn't strong enough for farm or factory work, Norm knew that if the government could use Papa in some way to help in the war effort, he would not hesitate to go.

But it was Etsu who left next. On a bitter cold February day, Norm and his brother and parents waited with her at the bus stop just outside the camp—but within view of a guard tower—for the bus to Salt Lake City. She would be marrying Mike on Valentine's Day. It was an emotional goodbye. Norm was happy for her, and glad that she didn't have to live in a camp anymore, but he was going to miss her.

Just before her departure, Etsu had enjoyed a special adventure.

A camp administrator who had befriended her wanted her to see Yellowstone National Park, which was close by. He got Etsu and another secretary out of the camp by having them hide under blankets in the backseat of his car. When Etsu returned that evening, she talked excitedly about Old Faithful geyser and the other natural wonders she had seen. She described such stunning beauty—mountains, waterfalls, hot springs, rock formations, and winter wildlife—that Norm was filled with longing to experience it for himself.

Now it was just Norm, Albert, Mama, and Papa. Mama made colorful pillows to create a comfortable back on Etsu's cot. It became an extra sitting space, helping to make their small room a little more homey.

In some ways, the camp was improving. The hospital, as one example, had been short on supplies and understaffed since its opening in late August of 1942, but was fully operational by March of 1943. Norm admired its tall smokestack, visible from all over the camp.

Even though the hospital was constructed of poorly built wooden barracks, and in spite of a shortage of doctors, the dedicated staff at the Heart Mountain hospital provided quality care.

Japanese American and white nurses worked together on the wards, but only white nurses could be supervisors.

The hospital had a staff of 150 doctors, nurses, dentists, pharmacists, nurse's aides, and orderlies. Some were internees, and they were paid far less than other staff members. A Japanese American nurse made only $19 a month, while a white nurse made $200 a month. It was that way with all the jobs in the camp.

Hospital staff treated the usual health issues, and also saw many bone breaks caused by falls on ice, burns from potbellied stoves, frostbite, and spider and snake bites. Along with transporting patients, the hospital's two ambulances delivered chilled formula to the barracks every four hours for new mothers, who had no way to refrigerate baby bottles.

Feeding newborn babies was only one of many challenges parents

These Boy Scouts are helping with the morning flag-raising ceremony.

in the camps faced. Another was keeping children busy and productive. When the children weren't in school, parents urged them to participate in sports, skill-building classes, and clubs and organizations started by internees. Especially Scouting, which had always been important in the Japanese American community because parents appreciated the Scouting commitment to self-improvement and to helping others.

Norm became a Boy Scout, joining Troop 379. He loved his new uniform, ordered from the catalog. He never missed a Scout meeting, and he worked diligently to earn merit badges, which his mother sewed onto his uniform shirt. When it was his troop's turn, he participated in raising the flag in the center of the camp early each morning, saluting smartly and pledging allegiance to the country holding his family prisoner.

Eventually the camp would have thirteen Boy Scout troops, four Girl Scout troops, and two Cub Scout packs.

Boy Scouts and Girl Scouts worked on merit badges of all types, from first aid and knot-tying to making and flying kites and volunteering at the Heart Mountain hospital. Weather permitting, Scoutmasters got permission to take Scouts outside the camp to fish, hike, and sleep under the stars. Some of the boys were in the drum and bugle corps and some of the girls formed a drill team, and together these groups participated in all types of special events in the camp.

Filling time was a problem for everyone; even adults with jobs had extra time on their hands. At Heart Mountain, as at all the other camps, the adults addressed this problem by sharing their professions, passions, skills, and hobbies with one another. Internees came from all walks of life—rich and poor, educated and uneducated, city people and country people—and they could learn from each other.

Musicians gave instrument and voice lessons, coaches organized sports teams and taught sumo wrestling. Artists led classes in watercolor, oil painting, pottery, and sculpture. Skilled needleworkers taught knitting, crochet, and needlepoint. Experts led classes on flower arranging, growing bonsai, jewelry making, woodworking, sewing, folding origami, performing traditional Japanese kabuki theater, and writing haiku and short stories. There was also a Japanese language class—which Norm carefully avoided—and classes in advanced English for Issei wanting to improve their language skills.

English was a popular course among the Issei because many had never had the opportunity to learn to read and write English.

There were dance classes of all types and weekly dances were held in block mess halls.

People formed bridge groups and played cards together for hours. Ping-Pong, chess, and checkers were also popular. Movies and plays drew big crowds. Recreation halls in two different locations served as theaters, one called the Dawn and the other the Pagoda. Going to the movies was one of Norm's favorite activities, just as it had been in San Jose. He liked every one he saw except *Citizen Kane*—he thought it was so scary that he left in the middle.

All the internees, especially the Issei, were pleased when the administration approved plans for a traditional Japanese summer festival to honor ancestors. It was something to look forward to.

Barber and beautician internees cut and styled hair. Engineers fixed electrical and mechanical problems, carpenters built furniture, and shoemakers repaired shoes. The administration started allowing restaurant chefs and short-order cooks to assist in the camp kitchens, and they worked magic with government-issued food staples. Even potatoes—served far too often to suit most people—tasted better when prepared and seasoned properly by Japanese chefs. Somehow they could even improve bologna and the ever-present macaroni and cheese. When more rice was finally added to the menu, everyone was happier.

"The improvement in food lifted our spirits," Norm said. "We had enough rice, and there was always tea to drink—though we all longed for Japanese-style stir-fried and fresh vegetables."

A solution was in the works. Among the internees were farmers, gardeners, and horticulturists who envisioned growing produce on the scrubland surrounding the camp. It would require water, plants able to tolerate the Wyoming climate, and a way to store harvested crops. The administration was supportive, hoping it would help the

These teens show off their moves, dancing to popular music at one of the weekly dances held in the camp.

Most camp administrators allowed internees to participate in traditional Japanese ceremonies like this Bon Odori festival to honor their ancestors.

camp to become self-sustaining. Already a camp farm run by internees was raising chickens, hogs, and lambs to supplement meager government meat rations.

The Shoshone River, named for the Eastern Shoshone of Wyoming, was a mile from the camp. Near it was an abandoned irrigation project, so with government-provided equipment and materials, crews of internees revived it. Despite poor weather, they completed a five-thousand-foot-long canal in time for the spring 1943 growing season. Internees cleared a thousand acres of sagebrush and rocks. Then they started planting, following guidelines drawn up by camp horticulturists who had done their homework, determining what to plant.

Area ranchers thought the project was foolhardy, insisting that

Internees watch as water begins flowing through the completed canal.

The irrigation canal and newly planted fields.

the land was only good for grazing cattle, and that the growing season was too short for any crops but sugar beets and soybeans. As canal water began to irrigate the fields and young plants started to poke their heads above ground, everyone waited to see what would happen.

CHAPTER 12

Baseball!

Baseball season also started that spring of 1943. As soon as the snow melted and the ground thawed, Heart Mountain's skating rinks were transformed into primitive baseball diamonds with homemade bases. The whole camp was mired in mud from spring rains, so leveling an infield was especially challenging. Norm helped to rake several of them, smoothing out the rough ground as much as possible. "It was a campwide effort," Norm said. "We all loved baseball, and everyone could be involved as a player, coach, helper, or spectator. I tried to play every day and I didn't care what position. When I was involved with a game, nothing else mattered. I was always trading baseball cards with other boys, and I watched for news in the *Heart Mountain Sentinel* about how my Cubbies were doing."

Papa shared Norm's love of baseball. Norm was surprised when he mentioned that it was also the national pastime of Japan and wondered how it got from America to Japan.

"When American missionaries brought us their religions, they also brought baseball," Papa said. "I felt at home in this country as

soon as I saw it being played here. Not knowing English didn't matter. Baseball has its own language."

The first internees arriving at Heart Mountain in August of 1942
had organized baseball leagues so that both kids and adults, male
and female, could play. Their baseball season was over by the time
the Minetas arrived that November. Now, because Papa was a block
chairman, he helped with organization and scheduling for the 1943
season.

Baseball and softball were popular at all ten internment camps,
and the *Heart Mountain Sentinel* regularly reported on how other
camp teams were doing. Norm loved reading that at Minidoka War
Relocation Center in Idaho the baseball team defeated the camp's military police team 14 to 1.

Girls and women played softball
as avidly as boys and men at
Heart Mountain. Several camps
had more than a hundred teams.
Parents appreciated that the
sport taught discipline and the
importance of being a team
player.

He also liked the story about an internee named Kay Kiyokawa (*Kee-yo-kawa*), who proved that the game could be a great equalizer. The Quakers had helped this young man leave the internment camp at Tule Lake, California, for the University of Connecticut, where he became a standout pitcher on the school's team. His first time up to bat, fans in the stands booed him, chanting "Hey, Tojo!"—a reference to the Japanese general so hated by American forces. He hit a strong single. His second time at bat, with fans still jeering, he hit a triple. But when he came to bat a third time, fans began chanting, "Slugger, Slugger!"

"Baseball helped all of us deal with our humiliation and anger," Norm said. "Every day, weather permitting, I knew I'd do something with baseball—watch it, play it, or just help out—and that made every day a good day."

When the new high school opened in May 1943 it had the best baseball field in the camp, with a real stadium, bleachers, and dugouts, compliments of the Wyoming Board of Education. The school budget covered the cost of new uniforms and equipment for the high school team. Other teams at Heart Mountain could use the stadium but had to raise funds to buy their own equipment and uniforms. Internees dug into their pockets to support their teams. Heart Mountain had several excellent ones, and large crowds always gathered to watch them play.

Since gasoline and tire rationing made travel difficult, camp teams mostly played each other or teams from area towns. Occasionally one of the camp teams traveled somewhere else. Usually the Heart Mountain boys returned victorious.

The best-known camp baseball team was at Gila River War Relocation Center in Arizona. The camp was constructed on scorching scrub desert and held thirteen thousand Japanese American internees. Like all the camps, it was rough and primitive.

The state of Arizona wasn't going to build a school baseball stadium in the camp like Wyoming had done for Heart Mountain. So an internee named Kenichi (*Ken-ee-chee*) Zenimura took on the challenge, creating a stadium that is legendary in Japanese American history. Zenimura was a five-foot-tall powerhouse baseball player who as a boy immigrated with his family from Japan to Hawaii. When he was twenty years old, he moved to Fresno, California.

Before the war Zenimura had organized a Japanese American all-star baseball team, the Fresno Athletics. He was a true baseball ambassador, taking several all-star teams to play in Japan, Korea, and Manchuria in the 1920s and 1930s. He helped break down the discrimination that existed in baseball in California against minority

In 1944 the Gila team came to play at Heart Mountain and won nine of their thirteen games. One game was called after two innings when a violent dust storm made it impossible to see the ball. Zenimura is the catcher in this photo.

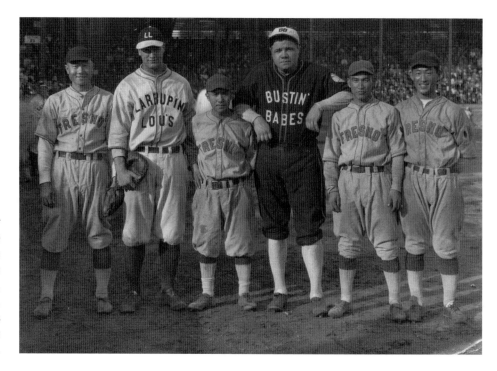

During a barnstorming tour of the West Coast before the war, baseball greats Babe Ruth and Lou Gehrig played in an exhibition game in Fresno, California, with Zenimura's team. In this famous photo, Gehrig is second from the left, Zenimura third, and Ruth fourth.

players, including Asian Americans, paving the way for them to later join the major leagues. He was also an excellent catcher and short-stop.

When Zenimura and his family were sent to Gila River, he vowed that he would build a stadium. Camp administrators okayed the project, probably thinking that Zenimura would give up. Instead, he drew up the plans and internees working with him found enough scrap lumber to build it. They even created a wall around it to stop fly balls by planting castor beans close together. The beans quickly grew so tall and so tightly interlaced that no baseball could penetrate them.

Then they diverted a water pipe three hundred feet from the laundry room to irrigate the playing field, creating a carpet of green grass. Internees donated money for uniforms and equipment, which had to be carefully inspected before games for scorpions and rattlesnakes. Thousands of internees attended those games, over-flowing the bleachers and standing anywhere they could find space. Coached by Zenimura, the Gila River team usually beat all challengers.

"We called Kenichi Zenimura the Dean of the Diamond and considered him the father of Japanese American baseball," Norm said. "He was one of my heroes."

CHAPTER 13

Meeting the Enemy

Late that spring, Norm's Scoutmasters decided that his troop would host a get-together with a Boy Scout troop from outside Heart Mountain. They reached out to troops in the area, but to their dismay, invitations were either declined or ignored. Then one said yes: Boy Scout Troop 50 in Cody.

When Alan Simpson, who was eleven and a member of Troop 50, heard the news, he wondered if it would be safe for the Scouts to go. Those people out in that camp were the enemy. They were Japs! Alan's cousin Bill Brady, a young navy pilot, had been shot down by the Japanese in the South Pacific in early 1942. Because his body was never recovered, he was considered missing in action. It was a horrible loss for the Simpson family—and the Japanese were to blame.

"Dad cried when he found out about Bill. It really unnerved me," Alan said. "I couldn't wait until I was old enough to sign up and go fight. I'd have done it right then if I could. My older brother, Pete, and I had a dartboard and we'd pin pictures of Tojo, Mussolini, and

Hitler to it and then throw every dart we had at that board as hard as we could, wishing we could just erase the whole war."

Alan's father, Milward Simpson, was a prominent lawyer in Cody. He had served in World War I, and he tried to enlist after his nephew's death but was told he was too old. Instead he signed up as civil defense coordinator for the county, a responsibility he took very seriously.

"In the first months after Pearl Harbor, we were all scared of a Japanese invasion, just like the rest of the country. We'd heard that the American Japs who lived along the West Coast were signaling them in," Alan said.

As part of the county's preparation, Alan's father arranged regular blackout drills. When the civil defense sirens went off, Alan and

Alan (second from left); his brother, Pete; and their parents, Milward and Lorna, in front of their home before a family bike ride. Milward Simpson served as governor of Wyoming and later as a U.S. senator.

Pete hurried through the house, turning out all the lights and pulling down the window shades. "We'd bought a special deck of cards that showed the silhouettes of Japanese and German planes, and we'd memorized all of them so we could identify and report them. We were always watching the sky. Pete and I both had .22-caliber rifles that we used for hunting, and we kept those ready, just in case," Alan said.

Monitoring air traffic was one way children could help with civil defense during the war. Flash cards, like this one, aided in identifying enemy planes.

"When the government said that an internment camp to house Japanese Americans was going to be built close to Cody, there was real concern. Dad thought that if the Japanese invaded the West Coast, we'd be sitting ducks because they would bomb us and then liberate the camp. Or what if the prisoners staged an uprising and got out? There would be ten thousand of them and only three thousand of us!"

Cody residents were shocked by plans to build an internment camp nearby.

As Alan would learn, residents of Cody and Powell weren't the only ones who were worried. The governor of Wyoming, Nels H. Smith, told officials in Washington that Wyoming people "have a dislike for any Orientals. . . . If you bring Japanese into my state, I promise you they will be hanging from every tree." Such racist sentiment faded somewhat during the construction of the camp, for it employed nearly two thousand area men for sixty days. A work crew could put up a barracks in six hours, spending less than an hour on construction of each room. Since some of the workers had little or no carpentry experience, floors, windows, and doors were often crooked. Green wood used to build the barracks was not properly dried first, so it shrank later, leaving gaps between boards.

"The camp went up so fast the summer of 1942 that folks around here felt like their heads were spinning," Alan said. "A whole city, ready to house ten thousand people, was created in just two months. The only towns in Wyoming that were bigger were Cheyenne and Casper."

Because of his civil defense responsibilities, Alan's father kept a close eye on the camp after it opened that August. He dutifully reported any rumors he heard to government authorities, including one that internees were being allowed to buy knives and other dangerous items that could be used in an uprising. That rumor concerned the FBI enough that a special agent was sent to investigate. He concluded that internees were just purchasing equipment they needed for work.

Milward Simpson also heard other rumors and complaints from area residents—that internees were being "coddled," that they had dishwashers and washing machines, that there was no food rationing at the camp like there was everywhere else, and that each prisoner was issued generous portions of prime beef and five gallons of whiskey. Of course, none of this was true.

Yet most folks admitted that Heart Mountain was good for the economy. In addition to the temporary employment of construction workers, several hundred people were permanently employed at the camp and made decent government salaries. Many area businesses also benefited. Dairy farmers increased their herds to supply the two thousand gallons of milk the creamery delivered to the camp each week. Other businesses contracted to provide such services as disposal of the camp's garbage, coal delivery, and laundry services for the administrative staff who lived at the camp.

In addition to a small group of internees who worked in the towns around the camp, others were occasionally issued one-time passes to take care of errands in town. Sometimes they were the targets of racist comments. A number of businesses, including several restaurants, refused to serve them. Tensions were always high whenever a local soldier died fighting against the Japanese, or when Japanese forces won another victory. "One business posted a homemade sign

The owner of this shop in Parker, Arizona, near Poston War Relocation Center, made it clear whose business was not welcome.

in the window that said 'No Japs allowed! You SOB's killed my son!'" Alan said.

Camp administrators tried to foster good relations with townspeople, but as one administrator said, "It was strange how the internees were great people when the locals needed their crops harvested, but once that was finished, they were 'dirty yellow rats.'"

Because of what had happened to his nephew, Alan said his father wrestled with his own feelings about them. He couldn't help but notice when he was at the camp how patriotic the internees were—some had American flags mounted to their barracks—and how polite they were. So when a delegation of internees approached him for help, he decided to listen. They told him that several Issei had died since arriving at Heart Mountain, and family and friends hadn't been allowed to include traditional Shinto or Buddhist rites and rituals in the burial services. Could he help?

He decided to try. He successfully lobbied the War Department, along with proper authorities in the Wyoming government, and secured the necessary permission. "Dad wanted to be fair," Alan said, "and he thought they should be able to respect their dead however they wished."

It was in a spirit of fairness that Alan's father encouraged him to meet the Scouts at Heart Mountain, telling him that he should see the camp for himself. Alan had to admit that he was curious to do just that.

But when the day arrived, Alan and the other Scouts were nervous. They had no idea what to expect. Scoutmasters Glenn Livingston, who was a school principal, and Bill Waller, a coach and teacher, reminded the boys that the Heart Mountain Scouts they would get to know pledged allegiance to the same flag and wore the same uniform. "We're going to learn about each other and we're going to have fun," they assured the boys.

"We felt better after that, so off we went, about fifteen of us, dressed in our Scout uniforms on a cold, overcast spring day," said Alan. "I was always the tallest kid and I had big feet. I also had a smart-mouthed comment for everything. I could be destructive—I got into a lot of trouble one time for shooting up mailboxes. But I usually behaved in Scouts.

"When we got to the gate at the camp, we had to be checked in by the MPs, and right away we noticed the guard towers and the barbed wire fence. We figured the prisoners must be pretty dangerous if they had to be guarded like that."

Alan's first surprise on entering the camp was seeing young children. "I thought, what are they doing here? They're just little kids! Yeah, they looked Japanese, but I knew they hadn't done anything wrong, so why were they behind barbed wire? That didn't make sense."

He was even more surprised when he met the Heart Mountain Scouts. "I don't know what I was expecting, except I was sure I'd recognize them as the enemy. I didn't even think they'd speak English. But these boys talked just like us and acted just like us. They had the same goofy grins we had and laughed at the same stupid jokes. The only thing different was their faces—and they weren't scary at all."

After preliminary rituals, the Scoutmasters paired up one Cody Scout with one Heart Mountain Scout for the day. As fate would have it, Alan was matched with Norm.

Their first task was to set up a pup tent. Because of recent rains, the ground was muddy, making this more of a challenge, but Alan and his new partner worked together well and quickly had theirs pitched. Then the group made beaded decorations to wear on their Scout kerchiefs and built a fire without using matches. Afterward they had a knot-tying contest. By then, Alan had long forgotten that Norm was the enemy. He was having way too much fun.

"As soon as we were paired up he started asking me questions. I liked to talk, so I was happy," Alan said. "I was a lot taller than he was and moved fast, but he kept up with me. We both liked the same dumb songs and talking about comic books, baseball, and our baseball card collections. We had a great time together."

After lunch in the mess hall, the Scouts had some free time. Alan was invited into one of the barracks by an elderly woman who smiled warmly at him. He took his muddy shoes off before he went in, and she showed him her family's small, crowded room. "Tell me about your family," she said. "Do you have a grandmother?"

"So I told her about my grandmother," Alan said. "And the whole time, I'm feeling something welling up in me because these people are living in tar paper shacks and they can't go home, and they're just so nice and I don't get it. How could I hate or fear them? I just couldn't."

When it rained in the afternoon, Alan and Norm stayed in their pup tent, telling jokes and sharing stories. Since he'd been thinking about his grandmother, Alan asked Norm about his grandparents.

"I've never met them. They live in Japan," Norm said.

"That's awful," Alan said. "You're missing out."

Norm nodded. "I envy my friends who have them close by. What are yours like?"

"My grandmother's beautiful and my grandpa is tough. He got mad at a banker who purposely bounced one of his checks, so he shot the man's ear off. That's how you evened the score back then. Buffalo Bill Cody started our town and was friends with my grandparents. Grandpa told me he came to their house once and serenaded my grandmother."

Alan liked that he'd impressed Norm, who seemed ready to listen to anything Alan wanted to talk about.

When it started raining especially hard, the boys dug a moat around their tent to keep it from flooding. Alan said that a Cody Scout who was a bully had his tent pitched down a slight slope from theirs. He convinced Norm to help him cut a channel in their moat to make the water drain toward the bully's tent, adding to his discomfort. "We laughed and laughed over that," Alan said. "I felt like I had a new friend."

At the end of the day the boys had to part. Norm would later describe Alan as very tall and a real smart aleck. "I'd have gotten in plenty of trouble if I talked like he did," Norm said. "I liked how he made everything we did together fun. I was sorry to say goodbye to him."

Alan felt the same. He was also confused and full of questions.

"I understood that we needed to defeat Japan in the war. That never changed," Alan said. "But after meeting the Scouts at Heart Mountain and seeing all those innocent people, especially those little kids, who'd had their liberty taken from them because of the way they looked, I had to rethink everything. That day I met the so-called enemy up close. I learned from Norman Mineta that we were both Americans and we were the same on the inside. We just looked different on the outside."

CHAPTER 14

The Miracle
of Heart Mountain

Working in the fields was difficult, but internees took pleasure in the crops they grew and the delicious meals everyone enjoyed as a result.

That summer, everyone at Heart Mountain was keeping an eye on the growing fields around the perimeter of the camp. Anyone who wanted to could be involved in caring for the crops. Norm and his friends often earned a few nickels helping out. Guards led workers to the fields and stood nearby as they tended the plants. "The guards didn't bother us," Norm said. "None of us was going to try to escape. There was no place to go."

One day Norm and Eddie had a close call. There had been many sightings of rattlesnakes around the camp, for warm weather had made them active. The boys had worked together that day digging up potatoes. They were leaving the field to return to camp when they heard the telltale warning of a snake shaking its rattle. They both froze.

"We knew you could die if you got bit, or at least get very sick," Norm said. "We'd been warned repeatedly to stay away from rattlers, but all these kids were around where the snake was, and I made up my mind right then that I had to kill it. I had a small knife with me—most of us had them because we needed them in the fields—so I decided to use it."

As Eddie watched in astonishment, Norm grabbed a stick lying on the ground that was shaped at one end like the letter Y. In one swift motion he pinned the snake's head to the ground with the stick and then stabbed it. To his amazement, it convulsed and died.

"I told my parents what I had done, and they were shocked. Thinking about it later, I realized what a risk I'd taken," Norm said. "But at the time, Eddie and I thought it was pretty cool."

When the boys got paid for their work, they headed to the camp store. It sold candy bars—Norm's favorites were Hershey bars and Baby Ruths—which cost a nickel. If he had enough money, he also bought a comic book—a bargain at a dime. He was always on the lookout for new editions of Batman, Green Lantern, and Superman. It pleased him that Mama and Papa allowed him to spend his earnings however he wanted.

One day he and Eddie joined an outing to hike up Heart Mountain. Norm was eager to experience the mountain up close and was also curious to see what the camp looked like from that high up.

"We took water and food with us and needed it," Norm said. "The

One of the most popular places at Heart Mountain was the camp store. Items for purchase included everything from canned and packaged food, to comic books, clothes, fabric, and craft items.

steep climb to the top and back was almost four miles each way. Papa had carved a walking stick that I used. It helped, but it was a long day and I was really tired when we returned."

During their hike the boys saw all kinds of birds, wildflowers, and ancient rock formations. "The leaders told us that the rocks were millions of years old," Norm said. From the summit they saw distant mountains with intriguing names like Sleeping Giant and a rock formation called Elephant's Head. The boys looked for a long time at the camp. "Compared to all that vast nature around us, it didn't seem very important," Norm said. "But the fields of crops were really impressive. Everything was lush and green."

Those fields yielded a bountiful harvest that summer, one so spectacular that it became known as the Miracle of Heart Mountain, for it produced over a thousand tons of vegetables. The harvest included wheat, barley, potatoes, corn, pumpkins, tomatoes, turnips, carrots, celery, cabbage, beans, and peas. Internees also grew daikon, a type of Japanese radish they considered a delicacy, and gobo, another much-loved root vegetable. Unfortunately, because the growing season was so short, the only fruit that did well was melons, but several types grew, including watermelons, which were very popular in camp.

Area ranchers became believers. Like most people in the Cody-Powell region of Wyoming, they hadn't been happy at the idea of

Fields with growing crops transformed the Bighorn Basin. In 1944 internees harvested 2,500 tons of produce—over twice the yield of the first year. The Shoshone River is in front and behind it are the fields, the camp, and then Heart Mountain.

having that "Jap camp" in their midst, but they had to admire what had happened: the arid Big Horn Basin around the camp was now vast, rich fields of produce.

"*Miraculous* truly was the word," Norm said. "We were very proud of what we had accomplished. Our chefs created the most delicious stir-fry and fresh vegetable dishes. They also pickled vegetables to make what we called *tsukemono* (*su-kay-mo-no*)—a traditional favorite that my parents liked."

To store excess produce, internees built three underground root cellars, digging them out with backhoes and then reinforcing them with wood and insulating them with hay. A pickup truck filled with vegetables could enter through above-ground doors and drive down a slope into each cellar. The largest of the three was over three hundred feet long—almost the length of a football field.

Trucks full of newly harvested produce used this entrance into one of the underground root cellars where food was stored, keeping it cool in summer and preventing freezing in the winter.

A Victory Garden was an outlet for creativity and supplied food and/or beautiful flowers. These tranquil spaces were also reminders of home.

Inspired by what was happening, many internees had planted small Victory Gardens, popular during the war as a way to grow food and flowers. Mama grew an array of colorful flowers outside the Minetas' barracks, contributing to the effort to brighten the camp.

"Some of the gardens were true works of art," Norm said, "and were inspired by traditional Japanese gardens. People would include

This photo was taken of the Minetas with friends shortly before Papa left for his government job. Min had come to visit for a few hours while on leave from the army to see Aya at Topaz, so he's in it too. Mama (on the left) and Norm (third from the left) are in the front row. Min (second from the left) and Papa (third from the left) are in the back row. This is the only photo taken of them at Heart Mountain.

interesting rocks they'd found and build small bridges over miniature streams. They were very creative. The peacefulness and beauty of our gardens and the abundant fields fed our spirits."

Early that summer Mike and Min joined the army. Even though Japanese Americans were not yet eligible for the draft, since the beginning of the war a small number of Nisei had stayed in the army or been recruited by the army to join as volunteers because they had unique skills the army needed. Mike would help form a special unit of Japanese American soldiers that would be called the 442nd Regional Combat Team and would serve in Europe. Min was fluent in Japanese and he qualified for the Military Intelligence Service. He went to work at a Japanese language school located at Fort Snelling in St. Paul, Minnesota. When Min left Topaz, Aya had to stay a few months longer until her paperwork could be processed.

Now the government recruited Papa to teach Japanese to enlisted men in the Army Specialized Training Program headquartered at the University of Chicago. It was a salaried position, and a prestigious one—another payoff of Papa's long-ago decision to become fluent in English. "We were very excited," Norm said. "Not only would we be leaving the camp, but Papa's job would put us close to Helen, who still worked as a secretary in downtown Chicago."

Norm's excitement was short-lived. When Papa requested that his family be allowed to leave Heart Mountain with him, he was told that the paperwork would take some time, just as Aya's had. So Helen found a small rental house in Evanston that she and Papa could share. This pleased Mama, for she knew that they would take good care of each other.

"It was extremely hard for Papa to leave us," Norm said, "but he finally had his opportunity to contribute to the war effort. Mama assured him that we would be okay and that we would see him soon. Papa didn't have to tell Albert and me to look after Mama. He knew we were very protective of her. Albert still studied all the time, hoping that by fall he would be off to college somewhere—something I tried not to think about."

In August, shortly after Papa left, Albert heard from the Quakers: he had been admitted to Drew University in Madison, New Jersey, to resume his premed studies. Just as his sisters and father before him, he said his goodbyes and then he was gone.

CHAPTER 15

Leaving Heart Mountain

It was lonely without Papa and Albert, but Mama was cheerful, keeping her focus on when the family would be together again. When school started, Mrs. Foucar was still Norm's teacher and she continued to help him with his reading and math. While he was gone during the day, Mama did housework and visited with her friends. They included Mrs. Hirano, their next-door neighbor from San Jose, who was also at Heart Mountain. She had recently learned that her husband would soon be released from the Department of Justice prison in North Dakota and would be allowed to join his family at Heart Mountain. He had never been charged with any wrongdoing.

Norm came straight home from school each day, knowing Mama would be waiting for him. "I was not quite twelve, but I was now the man of the family and it was my job to take care of my mother," Norm said. "This was the Japanese way."

Mama had become an avid knitter and made scarves and warm socks to send to soldiers. She knitted while Norm did his homework.

Sometimes he would take a break to roll the skeins of yarn into balls for her. Then they went to the mess hall to have supper.

They heard from Papa once a week. He wrote his letters in Japanese so Mama could read them more easily, and then she read them aloud to Norm. Papa reported that he was busy with his teaching and enjoyed it. He said that he and Helen were comfortable in their small house and they both commuted to their jobs on the elevated train, known simply as the "L." Albert also wrote. He was glad to be back in college and told them that the school had excellent labs and a first-rate science library. He had a nice roommate and was making friends. No one had used the word "Jap" around him.

The fall weather was pleasant, and time passed quickly enough. Norm hoped that by Christmas they would be reunited with Papa.

Then, in mid-October, he came home from school one day to find their room empty. Their neighbor, George Ichishita (*Ee-chee-shee-ta*), quickly appeared and told Norm his mother had been taken to the hospital in an ambulance.

Norm dropped his books and raced outside. The hospital was a mile away, up the hill on the edge of the camp. He ran as fast as he could, crying as he struggled against the wind. What had happened? Was Mama okay? If only Papa were here!

He arrived, breathless, at the front desk of the hospital and was directed down a long hallway to the women's ward. The hospital smelled of antiseptic. Everything was white: the walls and floors, the beds, the nurses' uniforms, and even the hospital gown his mother wore. Her eyes were closed. Next to the bed was an oxygen machine.

She opened her eyes and smiled weakly. "I've been worried about you, Norman. Are you okay?"

"Mama, you're the one in the hospital. What happened?"

"I don't know. They're doing tests."

"Did you get sick? Did you fall?"

"I suddenly had trouble breathing and had to sit down. I called for help and Mr. Ichishita came immediately. I've never ridden in an ambulance before. I will be all right, Norman. I'm just very tired."

He sat quietly beside her while she rested. He needed Papa here. The physician stopped by. He was Japanese American and told them he wasn't sure what happened but that it was probably the altitude, combined with all the dust, that had caused Mama's breathing problem. He explained that her heart had weakened and she'd have to stay in the hospital until she recovered—probably three weeks.

That evening one of the block managers arranged for Norm to call his father from a telephone in the administration building. Papa wanted to come immediately but the FBI would not give him permission. Norm never understood whether this was because they needed his teaching skills so badly or whether there was another reason, for Papa was technically free. He only knew that Papa couldn't come and he had to handle this by himself.

Every day he came home from school to an empty room and then made the trek to the hospital. He stayed with his mother until he had to hurry to the mess hall for dinner. Then he was alone in the room again. He did his homework. He kept Papa and Helen updated through letters, and they passed on the news to Aya, Etsu, and Albert. At bedtime he turned off the single light in the middle of the ceiling and tried to sleep.

"I had never slept alone in a room before and I felt very lonely. I worried about everything, like, what if the barracks caught on fire? Would I be able to get out? My parents had always taken care of me, and now I had to take care of myself and I didn't know if I could."

When the wind howled or he heard the cries of wolves and coyotes in the distance, he missed his parents even more. How could all of this have happened to his family? But he had no answer for that.

He learned to awaken himself on time so he wasn't late for breakfast or school. Mrs. Ichishita did his laundry. He tried to keep it minimal by wearing the same clothes several days in a row—something Mama never would have allowed. He went to the mess hall by himself and sat wherever there was a spot. People stopped to ask how his mother was, and family friends, especially Eddie and his parents, came by the barracks to check on him. The October weather had turned icy cold. On weekends, when he wasn't visiting Mama or doing chores, he skated with friends on the ice rink by the barracks until it was too dark to see. Even being outside in freezing temperatures was better than being in the room alone.

Mama was discharged the first week of November. She was weak from being confined to a bed for three weeks and was ordered to take it very easy until she was stronger. Neighbors gathered with Norm outside the barracks to welcome her when the ambulance brought her home. Norm was thrilled to have her back, but he watched her constantly, worried something might happen.

Several days later, Norm and Mama learned that they'd been given official clearance to join Papa: they would leave at the end of the month. Norm quickly shared the news with their barracks neighbors, who all crowded into their room to congratulate them. Norm could tell how happy Mama was. As for him, he felt like an enormous weight was being lifted from his shoulders. Soon Papa would be in charge again.

Right after that, they received even more good news. Because of Mike's military assignment, Etsu was going to move to Evanston to live with them. Helen had already gotten her a secretarial job at the same corporation she worked for. Norm and Mama were overjoyed.

On November 12, 1943, Norm celebrated his twelfth birthday. As he and Mama finished supper in the mess hall, San Jose friends presented him with a cookie holding a lit candle. They sang "Happy Birthday" as he made a wish and blew it out. Everyone discussed how wonderful it would be to leave the camp. They talked about the war, which stretched before them with no end in sight. Someday, they all said, they would be back together in San Jose's Japantown.

The days flew by. The Minetas had been at Heart Mountain for a year, and even though they lived in a single room, they had accumulated far more than Norm and Mama could pack into the suitcases they would carry. When she wasn't resting, Mama was sorting, packing, giving things away, and mailing items back to San Jose or on to Papa.

As the time to leave grew closer, Mama said she was ready. But Norm had mixed feelings. Heart Mountain had become his home. He had done well in school and would miss Mrs. Foucar very much—he'd never had a better or more caring teacher. He had experienced snow and learned to ice skate, he had killed a rattlesnake and had climbed Heart Mountain. He loved that mountain and would miss it. He would miss Eddie, too. And there were things he still wanted to do. He had hoped he might see Alan Simpson, the Boy Scout from Cody, again. And he wished he could visit Yellowstone National Park just as Etsu had.

But he was also eager to be reunited with Papa, Etsu, and Helen. He was glad to be done with the small room and all the cold and dust and wind. He longed to taste freedom and to no longer be confined by barbed wire and by guards with machine guns.

He wanted to live in a real house again, with a bathroom close by and a kitchen where he could get something to eat whenever he wanted and where Mama could cook all their favorite dishes. A house with a telephone so they could call Albert, and a washing machine so clothes didn't have to scrubbed by hand anymore. And he would be near Chicago, home of his beloved Cubs! But what he really cared about the most was being back with Papa.

The night before they left, he and Mama said their farewells to friends, tears mingling with excitement. The next morning—one of the last days of November—Norm and his mother made their way slowly down the sloped roadway to the camp gate, carrying their suitcases. The sky was cold and gray. Frost hung in the air and Norm could not see the mountain to say goodbye to it. After they passed through inspection, they were each handed $25 and their bus and train tickets—a token settlement the government gave anyone moving out of the camps.

Then they walked through the gate and down to the road to wait for the bus to Deaver, Wyoming, where they would take a train to Billings, Montana, and from there the train to Chicago. Norm had layered on all the clothes he could. His suitcases held the rest, plus his baseball card collection, his glove and ball, and his Boy Scout uniform. As they waited, he felt anxious about Mama. He was still the one in charge, and what if something happened to her while they were traveling? Who would help them?

Once he and Mama settled onto the bus, he realized that for the last eighteen months, both at Santa Anita and at Heart Mountain, he had usually felt safe. Now he was acutely aware of how much he and Mama stood out. Someone seeing their Japanese faces might think *Enemy Japs!* Norm knew that Americans were filled with more hatred toward Japan than ever. It was a small country, but it had a highly disciplined, effective military, and it was especially cruel to American soldiers and sailors captured in the Pacific.

Luckily, the trip went smoothly. They caught the train at Deaver and reached Billings that afternoon. Since they had a twelve-hour wait to catch the train to Chicago, they checked into a hotel across from the train station where they could stay warm and Mama could rest. For dinner they went to a nice restaurant next to the hotel. They sat in comfortable chairs at a table with a crisp white tablecloth and starched napkins. Norm could hear soft music playing somewhere. His mother told him he could order whatever he wanted, and he selected the deluxe hamburger and french fries. She chose fish and a salad.

When Norm finished, he stacked his dishes to take them to the kitchen. His mother touched his arm. "Norman," she said gently, "you don't have to do that anymore."

At 2 a.m. they caught the Chicago train. With gasoline and rubber tires rationed, people took trains whenever possible, and this one was packed. Uniformed soldiers on leave seemed to occupy at least half of every car. There were no empty seats, but a man offered his to Mama.

Eventually Norm got a seat several rows back. He kept his eyes on his mother. Almost everyone was smoking, and he worried that the smoke would make it hard for her to breathe. Several hours later, when the train made a stop and a dozen people got off, they were able to sit together, but they had to go to the dining car separately so they could save each other's seats. When it was his turn, Norm sat at a tiny table with his sandwich and bottle of Coca-Cola. He kept his head down, afraid of being questioned or called names—or worse, thrown off the train. He had heard stories of such things happening to Japanese Americans. But no one bothered him. He returned to his seat to find Mama asleep. He tried to sleep too, but even though he was groggy with fatigue, he could only nod off for a few minutes at a time.

Civilians wait alongside soldiers and sailors to board a train at crowded Union Station in Washington, D.C.—a scene repeated at train stations throughout the country.

Thirty hours after they had boarded the train, he came wide awake with excitement as they pulled into Chicago's Union Station. He anxiously searched the platform. What if Papa wasn't there? What if—but there he was, smiling and waving at them. It was one of the best moments Norm could remember. He hugged his father hard. At last! Papa was in charge.

The landlord had driven Papa to the station, and took them all home to Evanston. They had a warm reunion with Helen and Etsu, who were waiting for them. Their small bungalow was a converted two-car garage with a living room, a sunny kitchen with a breakfast nook, two small bedrooms, and a tiny bathroom. After living in a single room at Heart Mountain, it felt luxurious.

Papa said he and Mama would have one bedroom and Helen and Etsu the other. "You'll sleep on the sofa, Norman," said Papa.

Norm nodded. That evening he enjoyed his first bath since leaving San Jose, an episode of *Captain Midnight* on the radio, and a hot cup of Ovaltine. Then he settled into peaceful slumber. He was free.

CHAPTER 16

Victory Over Japan

Norm woke happy each morning. He reveled in simple things: going to the grocery store with his parents, talking on the telephone, having a radio again, turning on a lamp, making toast. Once more Mama had her own iron, and she ironed everything. The government was now Papa's employer and Japanese Americans were still not allowed to return to the West Coast, but no guard or barbed wire fence limited the Minetas' daily activities.

Though Norm longed for the day his family could go home, Evanston would do in the meantime. "I think we were the only Japanese Americans there. People looked at us with curiosity, but no one troubled us. When I entered seventh grade in December, I was the only Asian student in Haven Intermediate School. I had become so used to being surrounded by people who looked like me that this was a bit of a shock. None of my classmates had any idea that I'd just come from an internment camp, and I didn't tell them I was Japanese American."

But a few students suspected, and they wondered if he was a spy. "An article had appeared in a prominent magazine stating that

Japanese spies couldn't pronounce the letters *l* and *r*, so to find out, they'd try to get me to say words like *roll* or *later*. Of course, unlike Mama, I could pronounce them perfectly. I joked my way out of those situations, just like I did back in San Jose when all the problems began after Pearl Harbor."

One day in woodworking class a boy Norm thought of as a friend called him a "dirty Jap." Anger surged through him. "I whacked him on the hand with a piece of wood and it caused a bruise. I was sent to the principal's office and reprimanded, but I stood up for myself. I said that we all hated the Japs, that I was *not* a Jap, and that it was the worst thing anybody could call me. I was worried that I would get expelled, but luckily the principal took my side. I still had to sit in his office for the rest of the day."

Norm became close friends with Wally Schlep, who was a grade behind him in school. "Wally knew I was Japanese and he didn't care. We both loved baseball. He could recite the batting averages of at least a hundred players and he had one of the best baseball card collections I'd ever seen. We both loved the Cubs and I was thrilled when my folks let me go to Cubs games with him and some other boys. We would take the elevated train to Wrigley Field and sit in the cheap seats way over in the outfield. It was heaven."

Papa taught Japanese during the week in Chicago and on Saturdays. He wanted Norm to continue learning the language by studying it at home, doing the lessons that Papa used with his students. He insisted that once a month Norm attend his Saturday class. "Papa wanted me to have this connection with my heritage and to be proud of it," Norm said, "but I was a very reluctant student." It helped that on their way home they stopped at a Japanese market to pick up several delicacies for Mama so she could make Japanese dishes.

And for a while Norm had to endure the torture of piano lessons after Mama became friends with a woman who owned a piano. He disliked the piano as much as he had the violin. "Whenever I had to practice, I'd be looking out the window the whole time, wishing I was outside with my friends. Finally the piano teacher told my mother to save her money. Thankfully that was the end of music lessons for me."

Life away from Heart Mountain was almost normal for Norm and his family. But back at the camp the internees faced new challenges. Early in 1943, when the Minetas had still been at Heart Mountain, the government had required adults in all ten internment camps, including Nisei men of draft age, to fill out a long questionnaire meant to determine if they were loyal to the United States.

One of the questions asked if they would serve in the armed forces if drafted. Another asked if they would give up any allegiance they had to the emperor of Japan and instead swear allegiance to the United States.

Many people felt the draft question didn't apply to them because of their age and gender so they answered no. Some of the Nisei men of draft age felt that they shouldn't be drafted when their constitutional rights were being violated, so they also answered no. With the second question, some people, including Nisei males, reasoned that if they had never sworn allegiance to the emperor, why should they withdraw it? The Nisei who answered no were called the No-No Boys. Some of these Nisei as well as other people who had answered no were labeled troublemakers and sent to Tule Lake War Relocation Center, the government's high-security internment camp.

In January 1944, when the government officially changed the draft status of young Nisei men back to 1-A and declared them fit to serve in the military, five hundred Nisei from Heart Mountain either volunteered or were drafted into the army, many of whom were part of the 442nd Regimental Combat Team that Mike helped to form.

But there was also a group of Nisei men at Heart Mountain who refused to register for the draft. They were also called No-No Boys. They said that they were not afraid to go to war, but would join the military only when their constitutional rights were restored and their families were released from the camp. The government responded by sending seven of their leaders to Tule Lake and arresting sixty-three others, charging them with failing to register for the draft. They were put on trial in Cheyenne, Wyoming, in June of 1944, found guilty, and sentenced to three years in federal prison.

Refusal by Nisei men to serve in the military caused a rift in the Japanese American community. Everyone felt strongly about this issue. On one side were young men who stepped up to fight for their country. On the other were the resisters who took a stand on behalf of all internees by refusing to obey a government that had violated their constitutional rights.

In 1944 in the biggest trial in Wyoming history, sixty-three young men from Heart Mountain were convicted of draft evasion. President Harry Truman pardoned them after the war.

The controversy did not divide the Mineta household. "My father felt resistance was wrong," Norm said. "As always, his position was that we all needed to do whatever we could to support the war effort and show our loyalty. Later I took a more moderate view on this, but at the time I sided with my father. I also supported my two brothers-in-law."

Mike was now in Europe with the 442nd Regimental Combat Team serving as its public relations officer. Min was an administrator at the language school. Aya had joined him and they lived in Minneapolis.

Albert hoped to finish college before serving, unless he was drafted first. "I was secretly glad," Norm said. "It was bad enough having to worry about Mike."

The army was segregated by race, and the eighteen thousand Japanese American soldiers who served in the 442nd were led by white officers. Their motto was "Go for Broke," and they saw grueling action in France, Italy, and Germany. They helped liberate France. They also helped liberate the Dachau concentration camp in Germany—a fact that does not appear in official army military history.

In one famous incident, soldiers of the 442nd saved 211 Texas infantrymen known as the Lost Battalion. The Texans had been trapped behind enemy lines in France without food, water, or medical supplies. They were almost out of ammunition. For five long days, 850 soldiers of the 442nd advanced through heavy rain and fog, up steep terrain riddled with land mines, until they finally defeated the enemy and rescued the infantrymen.

Forty-two Japanese Americans were killed in the operation and several hundred were injured. Yet rather than acknowledge the heroic 442nd, almost all U.S. news sources simply said that the rescuers were American soldiers. But at least the governor of Texas

Soldiers of the 442nd Regimental Combat Team, shown here in France in 1944, were at the center of some of the hardest fighting of the war.

gave the 442nd special recognition, declaring them to be honorary Texans.

The 442nd became the most decorated unit in American military history; its soldiers were awarded almost 9,500 Purple Hearts, 350 Silver Stars, 4,000 Bronze Stars, 52 Distinguished Service Crosses, and 21 Medals of Honor.

While Mike was overseas, the family did its best to keep track of him. "We rarely knew where he was," Norm said. "We listened to the radio, subscribed to the newspaper and several news magazines, and watched newsreels at the movies. But it was hard to learn much since troop movements were classified."

Mike's letters to Etsu offered the best clues. She received one almost every day, since he could get them to her quickly through military mail. Military censors blacked out places and dates. "I used a magnifying glass, trying to see through the ink and piece everything together to figure out where Mike was," Norm said. "I had a map of Europe on the wall and I stuck pins in it to track his whereabouts. We worried about him all the time and really looked forward to those letters."

Mike stayed safe, but he had four brothers who also fought in the 442nd, and one was killed and another wounded.

While the 442nd served in Europe, other Japanese American soldiers also played a critical role in the war against Japan. After Pearl Harbor, when the army dismissed or demoted two thousand Japanese Americans already serving in the military, it also promoted in rank a select group fluent in both Japanese and English who became part of the Military Intelligence Service. Gradually the government had recruited another four thousand who were fluent in both languages. They were present at battles against Japanese forces and served as translators and interpreters and helped to decipher Japanese codes.

Their jobs were both secretive and dangerous. Several were shot by their own men who mistook them for the enemy. If they were captured by the Japanese, they were immediately executed. Some participated in daring escapades. There were stories of Japanese American soldiers getting close enough to enemy troops to pretend to be Japanese military officers and then ordering the troops to attack, sending them directly into American ambushes. Others went into caves located on Pacific islands where Japanese soldiers were hiding and talked them into surrendering.

Because of their work, Allied forces often knew exactly where the Japanese planned to strike next and were ready for them. Altogether it has been estimated that the assistance of these Japanese Americans saved more than a million American lives.

When Mike and Min went into the army, Papa and Mama put a small banner with two blue stars in the living room window—a sign that the family had two loved ones on active duty in the military. Blue stars were in windows all over America.

Unfortunately, so were many gold stars, which took their place if the loved one was killed in action. The Minetas stayed in close touch with friends at Heart Mountain, where five hundred blue stars sewn onto small banners hung in barracks windows. By the time the war finally ended, fifteen of the stars had turned gold.

On April 12, 1945, Harry S. Truman became president of the United States following the sudden death of Franklin Roosevelt. Less than three weeks later, on April 30, Hitler committed suicide. Germany surrendered on May 7, ending the war in Europe. The Minetas celebrated this great victory with all of America, thankful that Mike was unharmed and would soon return home. Norm completed eighth grade at the end of May, and Albert graduated from Drew University the same month. He immediately enlisted, and because he knew Japanese, he was accepted into the Military Intelligence Service and began training for the invasion of Japan. Everyone knew there would be great losses of life on both sides before the war with Japan was over.

"We were very afraid for Albert's safety," Norm said. "Mama was almost frantic with worry that the Japanese would bomb Albert's ship as it sailed to Japan. She was also fearful that our Japanese relatives would suffer during an invasion. We'd had no way to communicate with them since the start of the war and did not know how they were doing."

Albert was still making his way across the Pacific Ocean on a troop ship when American officials decided to employ a new weapon against Japan. On August 6 the world's first atomic bomb was dropped on the city of Hiroshima, incinerating eighty thousand Japanese and exposing tens of thousands more to the ravages of radiation poisoning. Three days later the Americans dropped a second atomic bomb on Japan, this time on Nagasaki, killing forty thousand people.

As with Hiroshima, Japanese Americans mourned the loss of relatives and friends when the atomic bomb was dropped on Nagasaki, shown here.

The American government was prepared to continue firebombing the small island nation. But Japan's leaders had finally accepted that they could never win the war. The suffering of the Japanese people had been severe. Hundreds of thousands had died or been injured in the war. Food shortages were everywhere. Multiple cities had been destroyed by bombs, including the two atomic bombs. The country might never recover from an invasion by the Allies.

On August 15, 1945, Emperor Hirohito of Japan unconditionally surrendered.

The war was over.

CHAPTER 17

Going Home

Fourteen-year-old Norm was visiting Min and Aya at their Minneapolis home when news of Japan's surrender came on the radio. Min and Aya now had two young sons, and for the second summer in a row Norm had gone to Minneapolis to help care for his nephews. He had traveled from Chicago by himself on the train. "I felt very grown-up, especially because what still seemed like a short time ago I had been a prisoner with no freedom to go anywhere," he said.

Norm and Aya danced around the room, laughing and crying all at once. They immediately called Papa and Mama, who were just as excited. Mama was almost faint with relief, for she did not have to worry about their relatives being harmed in an invasion, and instead of participating in that event, Albert would be part of the occupation of Japan.

Norm had just one question for Papa: when could they go home to San Jose? They had been gone over three years. But Papa didn't know. The ability to communicate with the Japanese in their own language would be crucial during the occupation, and Papa's current class of army officers would not graduate until the following spring. "We must be patient awhile longer, Norman," Papa said.

Norm returned to Evanston just in time to start ninth grade at Evanston Township High School in September 1945. He was upset to learn that one of his required classes was Latin. "Reading was a huge challenge for me in English. How would I ever learn Latin? I was certain I'd never pass the class."

Newspapers reported that the Japanese people were suffering many hardships after the war, including severe food shortages.

Albert was stationed in Japan's largest city, Tokyo, which had been fire-bombed by American forces for two days in March 1945, leveling much of the city and killing an estimated 100,000 civilians.

Mama and Papa were worried about all the Japanese, but especially their relatives. They urged Albert, who was stationed in Tokyo, to check on them. As soon as he had time off, he traveled three hours by train to Mishima. Mama's family, the Watanabes (*Wa-ta-na-bees*), received him warmly. They reminisced about meeting him for the first time when he was a small boy and had come to visit with his parents and three sisters.

Albert realized how little food they had, even though they were respected educators. He'd brought along several care packages Mama had sent, and promised to return soon with supplies he could purchase at the military base store.

The Watanabes gave him directions to the Mineta family home several miles outside of town. They loaned him a bicycle, and Albert strapped the rest of Mama's care packages to it and set off. He was dressed in his army uniform, for the military required soldiers to wear them at all times. As soon as he entered the countryside, people who saw his uniform ran away, terrified. Albert realized that he was the first American soldier they had seen, and they must have thought he would kill them. At the same time, had they gotten close enough, his Japanese face would have confused them.

He found Grandfather's house. As he approached the door he could hear people talking inside. He knocked. The voices went silent. No one answered the door. He knocked again. He sensed he was being watched, so he politely waited. He knew his uniform might have them worried since they did not know who he was. He continued to wait. Finally, forty-five minutes later, a boy opened the door and asked what he wanted. Albert smiled. "I am Albert Mineta, the number one son of the number two son of this household," he said politely in Japanese.

The boy went away. After another long wait he came back and

motioned for Albert to come inside. Following Japanese custom, Albert took off his shoes before he was shown into a formal room with a small low table in the center. He sat down cross-legged on one side of the table. Again he waited. He knew making him wait was a snub meant to show him his own unimportance. But why would he be treated like this by his relatives, since he had said who he was?

More time passed and then a door opened and Shigetaro (*She-gay-ta-ro*) Mineta, Albert's tall, bald, fierce-looking grandfather, came in. Recognizing him from photos, Albert stood up and bowed in respect, and then he and Grandfather sat down opposite each other. Albert introduced himself as the grandson who had visited as a small child many years ago.

Grandfather glared. "I always dreamed of seeing my American grandchildren again, but I never expected one to arrive in the uniform of the enemy," he said. He stood abruptly and left the room, refusing to speak further. Nor was Albert allowed to talk to anyone else in the family. The boy showed him to the door. Albert put on his shoes and departed, leaving the care packages behind.

But he didn't give up. He returned to Mishima on a regular basis to visit both families. He brought care packages and also food from the base store—scarce items like sugar, rice, ramen noodles, and cooking oil. At Grandfather's house he left these items with the boy. He always answered the door, and Albert now realized he was a servant.

Finally one day Grandfather appeared and gave Albert a curt greeting. The next time, he invited Albert inside and introduced him to his grandmother, his uncle, who was Papa's older brother, and his aunt and cousins. Soon Albert was a welcome visitor. Grandfather, a man of great pride, had been on the losing side of the war, but he had effectively humbled his American GI grandson.

• • •

Back in the States, it was time to close the internment camps. Administrators at all ten camps opened the gates and urged people to leave. Many already had—nearly twenty-five thousand of those initially forced into camps had already departed in the past three years for work, college, marriage, or the military, fanning out across the United States because they were not allowed to return to the West Coast. But more than ninety thousand remained—and many were reluctant to leave even if they could now return to the West Coast.

Norm understood, for he had also been fearful when he and Mama left. Camp was safe. The real world was full of dangers. The war might be over, but many people felt no sympathy for Japanese Americans.

Those still in camps carefully read the letters from friends who had already returned to the West Coast. The lucky ones were warmly welcomed. Locals had looked after their property and they had jobs waiting, allowing them to resume their former lives almost seamlessly. Others had mixed experiences. On Bainbridge Island there were now a few people who didn't want the Japanese Americans to be allowed to return. The first family that did found its farm vandalized and property stolen. But islanders quickly helped out with donations, and Quaker students from the University of Washington helped to get the farm in order and to prepare and plant the fields. Soon the family was back in business.

In some places Japanese Americans had nothing to return to. Their possessions had been stolen or destroyed and their fields and houses burned. Their farms, businesses, or fishing boats had been seized for nonpayment of taxes, and strangers now owned them. In just one of hundreds of such incidents, the six hundred families who stored their belongings at a Buddhist church in Los Angeles found that every single item had been stolen or destroyed.

Three-fourths of the returning Japanese Americans lost all or part of what they'd left behind. Some reclaimed their property, only to be terrorized in drive-by shootings or through anonymous threatening notes. Japanese American children returning to their old schools were bullied by students and even teachers, just as they had been in the days after Pearl Harbor.

"A national guard unit from Salinas, California, suffered heavy losses fighting in the Battle of Bataan in the Philippines against the Japanese," Norm said. "Some of the townspeople took out their feelings on returning Japanese Americans. There were firebombings, arson, and other bad things that happened. We still couldn't escape the fact that we looked like the enemy."

In various places along the West Coast, locals formed organizations like Seattle's Remember Pearl Harbor, which opposed the return of Japanese Americans. One of their signs read WE DON'T WANT ANY JAPS BACK HERE—EVER!

One family returned home to Seattle, Washington, to find this slur on their garage door.

At Poston War Relocation Center, internees lined up to get their ticket for the trip home.

In Washington, D.C., President Harry Truman wrote his friend Eleanor Roosevelt, "These disgraceful incidents almost make you believe that a lot of our Americans have a streak of Nazi in them." In spite of the president's sympathies, the government offered no assistance beyond giving anyone leaving the camps $25 and a bus or train ticket to their next destination—an insult in light of how much Japanese Americans had lost and how they had been treated. Many people felt the government should offer low-cost loans to help people get back on their feet, but this did not happen.

While Quakers and other volunteer organizations tried to assist with housing and jobs, there was only so much they could do. Money frozen in Japanese bank accounts had mostly been confiscated by the government and was never returned. Farmers had lost their land, and on the West Coast jobs were scarce or nonexistent. Businesses often hired returning veterans instead of rehiring Japanese Americans who had once worked for them.

For the older Issei, starting over could be impossible. Many had suffered greatly from harsh camp conditions and were no longer physically strong enough to work. The experience had broken some of them mentally, leaving them so depressed that a few took their own lives. Others had to rely on their children to support them—a disgrace for proud Japanese men who had always been head of the family and whose word had been law.

Those Nisei who refused to live in California or Oregon or Washington because they had been treated so badly there chose to start their lives over in other places.

So when some people still in the camps heard about the difficulties others faced upon their return, or learned that they had no homes to go back to, they wanted to stay where they were. They were used to living in the camps, and they had housing, food, and medical care. Why give it up?

Mama and Papa heard from friends at Heart Mountain that to pressure them to leave, the camp administration had closed the schools and shut down the newspaper. They had also halted field production and leased the land to area farmers. All of the farm animals and equipment had been auctioned off.

When administrators announced that the camp would close on November 10, 4,500 internees were still at Heart Mountain. Anyone who had not left the camp before then would be put aboard trains and buses back to their homes. That finally did it. A total of 14,025 Japanese Americans had been interned at various times at Heart Mountain.

Some of those who returned to the West Coast found that they had

The Sashihara family at Heart Mountain pack their suitcases to leave. Some internees had mixed feelings about going home.

lost their homes and ended up in temporary housing run by the government. Ironically, in addition to trailer parks, this included army barracks much like the ones they'd just left. Some would remain in such housing for years.

Papa assured Norm that their family would be all right. "I can rebuild my business and we will be stronger for this experience, Norman," he said. "No matter what else happens, we are very fortunate that Mike and Albert were not injured in the war."

The family knew that the college professor who had rented their house had taken good care of it. And friends who had already returned to San Jose awaited their return. Norm was eager to go.

Papa requested permission to resign from his teaching duties. When his resignation was accepted, Mama began packing. Several days before Thanksgiving, Norm said goodbye to his friend Wally and his Evanston classmates and boarded a California-bound train with Mama and Papa. Helen was staying behind with Etsu while she waited for Mike's return from Europe. Until he arrived, they would remain in the bungalow and work at their jobs.

Norm was very grateful to leave for California when he did. "Just as I feared, I was flunking Latin. I got out of there in the nick of time."

Internees at Heart Mountain say goodbye to those leaving for home.

CHAPTER 18

School, Army, Politics

On Thanksgiving Day in 1945, Norm and his parents arrived in Oakland, California. Instead of transferring to a train for San Jose, they were met by Ed and Betty Linderoth, the family friends who had taken them to the train freight yard in San Jose when they were evacuated in May of 1942. The Linderoths wanted to drive them the last sixty miles home.

Norm could barely contain his excitement as they pulled up to their house. Everything was happening just as he had dreamed it, and he almost cried with happiness. He went from room to room, drinking in every detail. His old bedroom was exactly the same, and it would be his alone since Albert was in the army.

Friends quickly filled the house. Eddie and his family were among the first. The Hirano family came from next door. Mr. Hirano did not want to talk about his time in prison, far from his wife and children, or even his time at Heart Mountain, where he had been reunited with his family after the Minetas had already left. "Forget about all that," he said. "The war is over and we are starting fresh."

The next morning Norm and his parents walked across the street to the Japanese Methodist Episcopal Church to check on their stored belongings. "Everything was just as we left it, including Mama's delicate china and her antique Japanese vases," Norm said. "We'd heard all the stories of people returning to find their property destroyed and their possessions stolen. But in San Jose the attitude was that 'our friends and neighbors are coming home.' Newspaper editorials had urged people to welcome us back. As a result, there were only a few incidents. Our things were safe. We knew we were lucky. We didn't take any of it for granted."

On Monday Norm started ninth grade at Peter Burnett Junior High School, happy to be back in school with Eddie and other old friends. He had thought that students and teachers would want to talk about the internment of Japanese Americans, but no one did. Perhaps they had decided that if they didn't mention it, then it hadn't happened.

This conspiracy of silence was everywhere, especially in the Japanese American community, and would last for many decades. "People felt deeply shamed that the government and the American people had thought they were helping Japan and needed to be locked away," said Norm. "Like Mr. Hirano, they just wanted to forget. In Japanese culture you don't discuss bad things. You don't share your feelings. We young people wanted to talk about it, but we knew not to bring it up."

Mike returned from Europe in early 1946. He and Etsu moved to Washington, D.C., where he continued his work with the Japanese American Citizens League. Helen moved back to San Jose to live with the family. She returned to secretarial work but still hoped to someday become a teacher.

Papa gradually rebuilt his insurance business and Mama rebuilt their comfortable home life. It took time for Japanese stores and markets to reopen, and she had to search out places to shop in the meantime. Very soon she was active again at the church and in the local Red Cross, and she attended every meeting of the PTA. The American occupation of Japan resulted in fifty thousand marriages between American soldiers and Japanese women, and Mama discovered a new passion: helping Japanese war brides in the San Jose area learn about American culture.

"My mother remembered how challenging it had been coming to a country where she didn't speak the language or understand how things were done," Norm said. "She wanted to help, so she would gather these young women in our home and teach them about American cooking, how to set the table, how to use silverware in addition to

Papa took this photo during a family outing in 1948, when everybody was together except for Albert. Left to right: Min, Aya, and their sons Keith and Larry; Mike and Etsu; Norm, then seventeen; Mama; and Helen.

chopsticks, and many other things. Her classes were so popular that she moved them to the church, where there was more room."

Norm's focus was school. He attended grades ten through twelve at San Jose High School. Because of his challenges with reading and math, he still had to work twice as hard as other students to get good grades, but he liked school. "We were fortunate to have excellent teachers who pushed us to think for ourselves," he said. "Some of them were war veterans who had a broad outlook on the world. I thought I wanted to be an aeronautical engineer until I took calculus and realized I'd never make it through a college engineering program, so I switched my interest to business."

He still loved sports, but he didn't make the track or tennis team. Even though he was short for a basketball player, he made the team "because I was a good jumper. I would start as the center, do the tip-off, and then leave the game." Away from school he played pickup

Norm (middle of second row) loved basketball. Since he wasn't as tall as most players, he practiced jumping until he could jump higher than anyone else.

Ansel Adams was famous for his landscape photography, but he also visited Manzanar War Relocation Center, where he photographed the camp and its internees, including these little boys sharing a book.

baseball when he had a chance, and the Cubs remained his favorite team. To make spending money, he delivered newspapers and in the summers worked as a fruit picker in fields surrounding San Jose.

His sophomore year he joined the school photography staff, covering events for the school newspaper and yearbook. Famed photographer Ansel Adams had a studio in Yosemite National Park, several hours from San Jose, and for three years, during winter break, Norm and the rest of the photography staff visited his studio. "He would critique our photos and give us pointers," Norm said. "I found out later that he had photographed the internment camp at Manzanar, but he never mentioned this around me."

Norm was a popular student, viewed by others as reliable, fair, a hard worker, a leader, nice to everyone, and funny. During his senior year in 1948 friends urged him to run for student-body president. "Because there was a lot of diversity in my school, me being Japanese

(*Above left*) Norm with his high school student council cabinet.

(*Above right*) Norm's high school graduation photo.

American wasn't an issue," Norm said. "Students didn't think it was a big deal when I won, but adults were surprised because it hadn't happened before."

His election even merited a few lines in a column in the *San Francisco Chronicle* newspaper. "The columnist mentioned something like, 'Isn't this interesting so soon after the war.' There was still a lot of anti-Japanese sentiment around, and I'm sure some folks weren't ready for it."

After high school Norm attended the University of California at Berkeley, majoring in business and minoring in transportation. "Getting people and goods from one place to another is at the heart of our economy. I found that interesting and wanted to study it," said Norm. "I couldn't have predicted how important it would be to my career."

When he learned that college fraternities were for whites only, he developed his own circle of friends. Helen lived nearby while he was a sophomore and junior. She was also studying at Berkeley to complete coursework for a teaching degree, because California schools no longer discriminated against Asians in hiring. "Mama was delighted that Helen could keep an eye on me," Norm said. "My friends found this amusing."

Norm was required to take Army Reserve Officers' Training Corps classes his first two years in college. America was headed back to war, this time in Korea, and odds were that Norm would be drafted. He decided to stay in ROTC so he could serve as an officer instead of a private.

In 1952 a new federal law eliminated race as a barrier to becoming a naturalized citizen, allowing Issei to finally become U.S. citizens. "My parents were very excited," Norm said. "They helped organize adult education classes in San Jose so Issei could prepare for the citizenship exam. Those who struggled with English could take it in Japanese.

"It was a very special day when our family gathered at the federal courthouse in San Francisco to witness my parents taking the oath of citizenship along with a large group of other Issei. Papa just glowed. He loved this country so much. Becoming a citizen helped take some of the sting out of the internment experience."

Norm graduated from college in 1953 and went into the army and was stationed in Virginia.

A fellow officer, a captain who was African American, was stopped for speeding. "Instead of being given a citation like a white person would be, he was arrested and jailed," Norm said. "In the South you were black or white in the 1950s, and I wasn't considered white. To escape the racism, I applied to go overseas."

In short order, Norm was accepted into the army's Military Intelligence Service, just as his brother Albert and Aya's husband, Min, had been. Because he had a working knowledge of Japanese, he was sent to Japan, which was still under American military occupation. Albert was no longer there; after serving in the army he had attended medical school and fulfilled his longtime goal of becoming a surgeon.

Norm was stationed just outside Tokyo. Though he looked Japanese, he felt like a tourist. "I didn't speak the language very well, and I acted and thought like an American. But I learned a deep appreciation for Japanese culture and how it shaped my family."

A few months after Norm arrived in Japan, Mama came to visit and was eager to introduce Norm to his Japanese relatives. "My grandparents were no longer living, but I met aunts, uncles, and at least twenty cousins, including one who had fought for Japan in the war. These relatives had never seemed real to me—they were just images I had seen in photos. Now I had this whole new family and it was truly wonderful."

Norm began learning about his family history and developed pride in his ancestry. The Minetas could trace their history back nine hundred years and were descended from samurai. So were Mama's family, the Watanabes, who had drawings of their samurai ancestor and still owned one of his ceremonial swords. Norm found all of this intriguing.

He had thought that the Minetas were dirt farmers. "But they were actually the owners of a prosperous tea and strawberry farm," he said. "Papa had a comfortable childhood."

After Japan, Norm served as an intelligence officer in South Korea and finished his military service in 1956.

He had just returned to San Jose when Mama had a stroke. She died two days later at age sixty-four. The family was heartbroken. "That was the third time I saw my father cry," Norm said. The other times had been after Pearl Harbor and the day the family was forced to leave San Jose.

With Mama gone, Helen moved in with Papa to look after him. She was a teacher at long last, teaching American history classes at San Jose High School, where she would remain the rest of her career. Norm lived nearby and soon joined the Mineta Insurance Agency, just as Papa had always hoped he would. Not long after, he met May at church. She had recently moved to San Jose. As a child she had been interned with her family at Amache War Relocation Center in Granada, Colorado.

When this photo was taken of Norm in South Korea, he and two army friends had just returned to headquarters from field operations. Norm is on the left.

"Before the war her father had a very successful laundry and dry-cleaning business. He was even a member of the Rotary Club, which was almost unheard of for an Issei back then," Norm said. "But the internment experience left him too broken to restart his business, and he died shortly after the war."

Norm and May were married and became the parents of two sons, David and Stuart. Along with work and family, Norm was active in church and community organizations. He was asked to fill a vacancy on the city's Human Relations Commission, which led to an appointment on the Housing Authority board. Then the mayor and city council appointed him to fill an empty seat on the council. In 1969 he ran for office for the first time, winning a four-year term on the council. He was subsequently appointed by the other members of the council to be vice mayor.

"Papa had always stressed the importance of giving back to the community, and he was proud of what I was doing," Norm said. "But he was also concerned about the responsibility I was taking on. The work was hard, but it was also rewarding."

From the beginning of his political career Norm encouraged minorities to run for office, telling them, "All of us need representation when the decisions are made. In the camps we didn't have anyone to advocate for us because our leaders had been arrested. As a politician I have tried to speak out for those who needed representation and to make a difference for them. You can do that, too." He also urged protesters to run for office. "Don't just make noise," he said. "Do something positive."

Norm was a popular councilman, and in 1971, at age forty, he was elected mayor. "I don't know if this could have happened anywhere else," he said. "San Jose was such a special place because of its diversity. My race was never discussed."

Though he did not know it at the time, he was the first Asian American to be elected mayor of a major American city. A story went out on the news wires, and a short time later an envelope arrived in the mail with a Cody, Wyoming, postmark.

Norm was amazed. "Twenty-eight years after we'd shared goofy jokes in a pup tent at Heart Mountain, I was reading a note of congratulations from Alan Simpson."

CHAPTER 19

A Distinguished Career

Norm wrote back to Alan, recalling the day they met at Heart Mountain. "He had asked in his note if I remembered him, and of course I did. You don't forget Al Simpson."

Norm worked hard as San Jose's mayor, tackling housing, transportation, and other major issues affecting the city. In 1974 Papa died at age eighty-six, leaving a hole in Norm's life as big as the one left by his mother's death. "My parents were the most influential people in my life," he said. "I was so fortunate growing up in that household."

That same year he made his first run for national office, winning a seat in the U.S. House of Representatives. His mentor was Daniel Inouye from Hawaii, the first Japanese American to serve in Congress. Inouye, who lost an arm fighting with the 442nd in the war, was elected to the House of Representatives in 1959 when Hawaii became a state. Hawaiians elected him to the Senate in 1962.

Norm was so well liked by California voters that he was reelected to the House nine times, serving a total of twenty years. In 1978 Alan Simpson, then a lawyer in the Cody law firm started by his father,

This photo shows Norm as a newly elected congressman in 1974. One of the important bills he helped sponsor was the Americans with Disabilities Act of 1990.

joined Norm in Congress as a senator from Wyoming. "It was a great day when we met up in Washington," Norm said. "He was six foot seven inches tall and slimmer than I remembered. He was still mouthy and funny, with a joke for every occasion. I was sure glad to see him again."

They were political opposites—Norm a moderate Democrat and Alan a conservative Republican—but something clicked, just as it had at Heart Mountain. Soon they were getting together socially outside of work, or meeting for lunch at the Capitol. When they disagreed, they were open about it. Sometimes one of them would even change his point of view.

Both men earned reputations for taking on civil rights issues. They formed a powerful alliance, working across party lines to pass several important bills. When Norm mentioned seeking justice for the internment of Japanese Americans, Alan was immediately on board. "Anything connected with racism, I wanted in," he said.

Etsu's husband, Mike, who still worked for the Japanese American Citizens League, had been instrumental in getting Congress to pass a bill in 1948 to allow Japanese Americans who had been interned to apply for losses of property. Only a quarter of the resulting claims were approved because it was so difficult to qualify. But by the 1970s support was building within the Japanese American community to seek two things: an apology from the U.S. government, and restitution in the form of a cash payment to internees to help offset all they had lost. Proponents felt that this was an issue that affected every American, for if one group could be singled out and treated unjustly, then every group was at risk.

In the late 1970s, Mike had already left the JACL to start his own business when the organization approached Norm and the three other members of Congress who had Japanese ancestry to begin the work. The first task was convincing Congress to appoint an official body to review the facts. They did, and the Commission on Wartime Relocation and Internment of Civilians concluded, after public testimony and thorough study, that the internment of Japanese Americans was the result of "race prejudice, war hysteria, and a failure of political leadership." The commission recommended that each living internee receive $20,000 in restitution.

First elected to the Senate in 1978, Alan Simpson served eighteen years in the Senate, ten of them as the second-ranking senator in his party.

Next, Norm and Alan introduced a bill in Congress seeking both the payments and an apology. Four times it was defeated, and each time Norm reintroduced it in the next session. He made certain that it always carried the number H.R. 442, in honor of the 442nd Regimental Combat Team.

While he worked in the House to get needed cosponsors, Alan did the same in the Senate. When senators protested that internment hadn't been wrong or that it hadn't been so bad, Alan said, "I told them in no uncertain terms exactly what had happened. I was there. I saw it."

When the notion of paying survivors was criticized, Norm defended it in his testimony during a hearing. "Would I sell my civil and constitutional rights for $20,000? No. But having had those rights ripped away from me, do I think I am entitled to compensation? Absolutely."

Norm also reminded members of Congress that two-thirds of the internees were American citizens and one-third—the Issei—had been denied the right of citizenship for racist reasons, but that even if they had been citizens then, their constitutional rights would have been ignored. "Our own government had branded us with the unwarranted stigma of disloyalty which clings to us still to this day," he told his colleagues. "So the burden has fallen upon [Congress] to right the wrongs of forty-five years ago." The bill was passed by the House of Representatives in 1987 and the Senate in 1988.

Alan helped persuade President Ronald Reagan, a fellow Republican, to sign the bill into law. It became known as the Civil Liberties Act of 1988. Norm has always considered his contribution to its passage to be his greatest professional achievement. At the signing ceremony the president recounted the story of what had happened to Norm and his family.

Restitution began in 1990 when the oldest camp internee, who was 102, received the first check. Another 82,219 internees also received checks, along with a letter of apology from then-President George H. W. Bush, that said in part, "We can never fully right the wrongs of the past. But we can take a clear stand for justice and recognize that serious injustices were done to Japanese Americans during World War II."

"For decades no one spoke about the camps and what they suffered," Norm said. "My parents and so many others were silent, shamed by what had happened to them. For many, healing began when the Civil Liberties Act was signed into law."

Norm wished Papa and Mama had been alive to celebrate with the Japanese American community, but he was grateful that Aya, Etsu, Helen, and Albert could share this momentous victory. Helen died in her late seventies, but Aya, Etsu, and Albert all lived into their nineties and Norm remained close to each one of them. Until her death,

President Ronald Reagan signed the Civil Liberties Act on August 10, 1988, as Norm, second from left, looked on.

he also stayed in touch with Mrs. Foucar, his teacher at Heart Mountain, visiting her at her Denver home whenever he could. "We talked about why she had come to Heart Mountain to teach. She had wanted to do her small part to help, she said, because she felt strongly that what was being done to us was an injustice. She made a big difference in my life."

In 2000, when Norm was easing into retirement, President Bill Clinton asked him to be his secretary of commerce. Norm accepted, becoming the first Asian American appointed to a Cabinet position. Many evenings found him working late because there was so much he needed to read, and he still read slowly.

In 2001 he came close to witnessing injustice yet again. That was his first year as secretary of transportation in the George W. Bush administration—the only Democrat in an otherwise Republican Cabinet. On September 11, when Arab extremists killed three thousand Americans in terrorist attacks, the public wanted revenge. Calls went out to ban Muslims and people of Middle Eastern appearance from boarding American planes.

"I wanted to make sure this rhetoric did not catch on," Norm said. He sent a memo to the airlines forbidding them to pull aside travelers for extra security based on appearance. In a speech to the American public, President Bush, knowing Norm's story, urged that Muslims and Middle Easterners not be blamed for the actions of radicals, citing the internment camps and what happened to Norman Mineta.

In the ensuing months Norm oversaw the creation of the Transportation Security Administration's airport security system. "People complained that TSA agents were checking toddlers and grandmothers in wheelchairs, but it was very important that we treated everyone equally," he said.

Norm was secretary of transportation from 2001 to 2006. He

worked in the private sector for several years after that, and then finally retired. Today he continues to volunteer with a variety of organizations and serve as a consultant to various government groups. He attends meetings all over the country, but especially in Washington, D.C., and lives an hour from there with his second wife, Deni. He and May had divorced long ago, and when he met Deni they each had two adult sons. Today they share eleven grandchildren.

One event dear to them is the Heart Mountain Pilgrimage that takes place each summer at the site of the internment camp—now a national historic landmark.

"Some very impressive and hardworking folks in the Japanese American community got the ball rolling on this," said Norm. They formed the Heart Mountain Wyoming Foundation to purchase the land, then in private hands. Both Norm and Alan, now honorary

Norm and Deni were married in 1991 in the chapel of the U.S. House of Representatives in Washington, D.C. Left to right are Norm's son David, Min and Aya, Norm's son Stuart, Deni and Norm, Helen, Albert, and Etsu and Mike.

advisers to the foundation, helped to raise $17 million in private funding to build the Heart Mountain Interpretive Center near the old entrance to the camp.

The first three-day Heart Mountain Pilgrimage was held in 2012 to bring together survivors and their descendants, supporters, and the general public to commemorate what had happened there and to further an understanding of why. The pilgrimage and the interpretive center have helped families discuss for the first time the impact that internment has had on generations of Japanese Americans.

"Young Japanese Americans are sometimes critical of the older generations for not standing up for their rights," Norm said. "They'll ask, 'Why didn't you fight back?' But our culture was to obey authority. We were loyal to the government and we felt we must prove it by doing what we were told. Coming to Heart Mountain, just being in that place and hearing the stories of what happened there, younger family members understand, often for the first time, what we experienced and the shame that we endured.

"When you visit the center and tour the site, you realize how important it is that we be vigilant. We can never assume that the government will do the right thing. The Fifth Amendment to the Constitution guarantees that 'No person shall be deprived of life, liberty, or property, without due process of law.' But there was no due process for Japanese Americans during World War II. Ever since 9/11, there's been anti-Muslim and Middle Eastern rhetoric—talk of a national registry, roundups, camps, and deportations. We cannot allow this to happen again. Not to them, or to anyone seeking refuge here, including those who cross our southern border, and others fleeing war-torn countries around the globe."

The Minetas and Simpsons meet up each summer at the Heart Mountain Pilgrimage, and a couple of other times each year. They have traveled the world together. "He's a river running deep," Alan said of Norm. "I love the guy. When we get together we hug and kiss and our wives roll their eyes, but that's just how it is. We joke and laugh and have a lot of fun, but if you put something big in front of him that needs doing, he'll get right to work. He's a careful thinker, thoughtful, savvy, and smart, and he's helped change this country for the better."

One key to the unlikely friendship between Norm and Alan is that they get great pleasure from making each other laugh.

Norm envisions this country as a tapestry. "We often liken America to a melting pot where we blend together, giving us one identity," he said. "But I think our strength is rooted in our differences. We are all strands of yarn—different textures, different colors—and woven together, we make a strong, integrated whole.

"Every four years when teams march into the Olympic stadium, you already know what the athletes from Japan, Norway, or Ethiopia will look like, but the U.S. team is all these strands of yarn. It always gives me a thrill. My own family is a mix. My wife is white. One of my sons is married to a Chinese American and the other to a Nicaraguan American. Let's embrace and celebrate our differences.

"There were good citizens who didn't rise up to protest what was happening to their Japanese American friends and neighbors in 1942. But if we will speak out when we see someone's constitutional rights being violated, if we will act together, then we are strong enough to withstand any evil, internal or external, that threatens to unravel this beautiful tapestry that is America."

Additional Information

Selecting the Right Terms

Were Japanese Americans *forcibly removed, evacuated, relocated, detained,* or *deported*? Did they go to *internment camps, prison camps, detention camps,* or *concentration camps*? Were they *internees, detainees, evacuees, incarcerees,* or *prisoners*?

And is *Japanese American* a proper term? Two-thirds of those rounded up were American citizens, so technically they were Americans who happened to have Japanese ancestry, just as another citizen might be an American who happened to have Swedish ancestry. Should the Issei be referred to as Japanese Americans when they were not American citizens? For the sake of convenience, I've used the term *Japanese Americans* to refer to both Issei and Nisei in this book, though some authors do not.

Norm and I debated about all this and also about other terms used here. During World War II the government referred to the camps as *concentration camps,* but out of respect for those who suffered so grievously in the Nazi concentration camps, we chose not to use that term. *Internment, evacuation, detention,* and *relocation,* on the other hand, could sound like voluntary displacement. *Prison camp* and *prisoners* are accurate terms, but because they are not commonly used in references to the Japanese American experience, we have primarily used the terms *internment camp* and *internees.*

Honoring Norman Mineta

Norman Mineta has been honored numerous times for his contributions both to the United States and to Japan. He has worked tirelessly to promote closer relations between the two countries, helping to found the Congressional Asian Pacific American Caucus for this purpose. In recognition of his work, in 2007 the Japanese government awarded him one of its highest honors, the Grand Cordon of the Order of the Rising Sun.

By then the U.S. government had already honored him with its highest civilian award, the Presidential Medal of Freedom. His many other honors include the Distinguished Medal of Honor for Lifetime Achievement and Public Service from the Japanese American National Museum, where he has served as chairman of the board of trustees. He is a former regent of the Smithsonian Institution. San Jose has recognized its native son several times. Its airport is named the Norman Y. Mineta San Jose International Airport, and San Jose State University is home to the Mineta Transportation Institute. California State Highway 85 also bears his name.

Batting a Home Run

When Norm was still a congressman, a wealthy businessman heard him tell the story of his bat being taken from him the day his family left for the assembly center. He sent Norm a bat signed by two of the greatest baseball players in history: Hank Aaron, America's home-run king, and Sadaharu Oh, Japan's home-run king. Norm was thrilled, but he had to return it; legislators could not accept gifts worth more than $250, and the bat was worth much more. He joked to a reporter that "the damn government took my bat again!" When he retired, the businessman again sent him the bat. It has hung in Norm's office ever since and is one of his prized possessions.

Rounding Up Others

At the start of World War II, an estimated four hundred thousand people with Japanese ancestry lived in the Western Hemisphere. Canadian authorities imprisoned twenty-two thousand Japanese Canadians in camps set up in ghost towns and on farms. Just over two thousand Japanese living in Peru and Latin America were sent to camps in the States.

When Japanese forces invaded two of the islands that were part of the Aleutian archipelago off the coast of Alaska, the U.S. evacuated 881 islanders from nine villages in the Aleutian chain and the Pribilof Islands, supposedly to protect them. Then they burned most of the islanders' villages, making them useless if the Japanese invaded. The islanders were sent to primitive camps near Juneau, Alaska, two thousand miles from their homes. They suffered greatly before they were allowed to return home and begin the difficult task of starting over.

Imprisoning Orphans and Foster Children

Children living in orphanages or foster care who had Japanese ancestry did not escape internment. Government officials combed through child placement records in the evacuation areas, searching for children who were one-eighth or more Japanese. Some of the ones identified were unaware of their Japanese ancestry. Half were under the age of seven. Most were in care facilities in the Los Angeles area.

From babies to teenagers, they were rounded up and put aboard buses under armed guard for the trip to Manzanar War Relocation Center, two hundred miles northeast of Los Angeles. Frantic over what would happen to the children, several Japanese American staff members from the orphanages begged for permission to go along to care for them. From June 1942 to September 1945, a total of 101 children lived in what was called the Children's Village. It had three barracks: one for girls, a second for boys, and a third for staff.

When Manzanar closed at the end of the war, the children were once again placed in orphanages and foster homes. The story of Manzanar's Children's Village has remained largely unknown, for like many of the internees, the children chose not to discuss it, even as adults.

Children who were already in orphanages or foster homes were further traumatized when they were interned at Manzanar War Relocation Center, even though they posed no security threat to the country.

Staying Together

Mixed-race couples had to decide if the non–Japanese American spouse would also be interned. Heart Mountain had about a dozen mixed-race families. In several, the non–Japanese American father or mother did not live in the camp with the family, but instead worked at a job elsewhere and visited whenever possible.

Perhaps the best-known non–Japanese American spouse at Heart Mountain was Estelle Peck Ishigo (*Ee-shee-go*), an artist whose drawings have helped to illustrate what daily life was like for internees, several of which are in this book. (*http://encyclopedia.densho.org/ Estelle%20Ishigo/*)

Waging Peace

During World War II, Quakers, who are members of the Religious Society of Friends, were devoted to helping those in need. In Europe they helped refugees escape the Nazis, and assisted in getting Jewish children to safety in other countries. While unwilling to fight in the war, young Quaker men also served as medics and ambulance drivers, some sacrificing their lives.

In America, Quakers helped Japanese Americans in many ways, providing moral support, food, and all kinds of practical assistance. At some of the camps they pressured administrators to improve conditions. They worked tirelessly to help internees like Norm's brother, Albert, get into college, and as a result, more than four thousand internees left the camps to attend some six hundred institutions of higher learning. The Quakers also helped thousands of internees find jobs that got them out of the camps and helped ease labor shortages across the country. As Norm knew so well from Mrs. Foucar, some Quakers also relocated to become teachers in the camps.

When the war ended, Quakers helped Japanese Americans find jobs and housing—no easy task in a country still roiling with anti-Japanese hostility. In Europe they assisted displaced persons struggling to find family members and to create new lives for themselves. They also assisted Japanese victims of the bombings of Hiroshima and Nagasaki.

They did these things because they opposed violence in any form. Today, as then, they seek to help all victims, regardless of who they are or which side of an issue or a war they might be on.

Most Japanese Americans viewed the selflessness of Quakers as heroic, and when they learned that the Friends societies in England and America were jointly awarded the Nobel Peace Prize in 1947, they welcomed the news.

Writing to Miss Breed

When the roundup of Japanese Americans began in San Diego, California, Clara Breed worried about the children she knew from her work as the children's librarian at the San Diego Public Library. She kept in touch with many of them via mail while they were in the camps. In addition to writing them newsy letters, she sent them care packages with books, candy, and other items. She saved the letters they wrote to her, many of which appear in the book *Dear Miss Breed* by Joanne Oppenheim. The letters bring to life day-to-day happenings in the camps. The Japanese American National Museum in Los Angeles has the entire set of letters in its collection.

Living in the Camps

Scorpions, rattlesnakes, blizzards, and blazing heat were among the challenges faced by internees in the ten permanent internment camps. One could easily believe that the government had picked the worst locations it could find. Nine were constructed on government property, including two on Native American reservations. All were in sparsely populated areas, supposedly to protect the internees—but also to make certain they were no threat to the public. All ten were inhospitable in one way or another. They were too hot or too cold. Some had terrible dust storms or heavy winter snows. Two were surrounded by swamps and infested with flies, mosquitoes, snakes, and scorpions. Several had hard, rocky soil and no nearby water source.

The National Park Service, working with grassroots organizations, has helped to preserve what remains of those on public lands, and in many instances the sites have been declared national historic landmarks.

An internee arriving at **Manzanar War Relocation Center** in central California said, "All we could see was sand with sagebrush and tumbleweed blowing in the wind on both sides." It was so bleak that "even some of the soldiers who escorted us . . . had tears in their eyes as they left us." Internees had to adjust to freezing, damp winters and hot, dry summers. "We slept in the dust, we breathed the dust, and we ate the dust," said another Manzanar internee.

Manzanar is now a state park and a national historic site. It was the first of the camps to host an annual pilgrimage. Visitors can tour the interpretive center and pay tribute to the Japanese Americans who were incarcerated there.

There was no lake at **Tule Lake War Relocation Center** in northern California, ten miles from the Oregon border. It was a bleak, difficult maximum-security facility where "troublemakers" from the other camps were sent. Tight security included eight-foot fences and more than a thousand military police guards manning machine guns, tanks, and armored cars. The camp included a jail and stockade area.

Barracks were searched regularly, and some internees were deported to Japan. Part of the site is now a national historic landmark.

Granada War Relocation Center, known as **Amache**, was the smallest of the camps. In spite of strong anti-Japanese sentiments in Colorado, the state's governor, Ralph Carr, offered his support to the camp. Internees encountered only minimal hostility from local farmers, who needed their help in the fields. When the sugar-beet harvest was threatened, volunteers from the camp worked alongside paid laborers to save it.

Because of friendly relations with locals, internees were free to walk to the little town of Granada, a mile away, to shop and eat. Merchants stocked special food items for them such as soy sauce. They also hired internees to work for them, and in many instances became their friends.

Today, visitors to the site of the camp pass through barbed wire at the original entrance. They can see artifacts from the camp at the Amache Museum in downtown Granada.

When internees first arrived at **Gila River War Relocation Center**, in Arizona, strangers had to share rooms in the unfinished barracks. The camp was located on the Gila River Indian Community reservation, and the government kept Native Americans and internees apart. Temperatures ranged from -30 degrees in the winter to as high as 125 degrees in the summer. Dust clogged everyone's lungs, creating serious health issues. Keeping clean was impossible. Most internees slept outdoors during hot spells.

Gila was notable for a successful agricultural operation that not only fed the camp but also produced millions of pounds of produce that was shipped to other camps. It was at Gila that Kenichi Zenimura built his baseball stadium. First Lady Eleanor Roosevelt visited Gila in 1943, drawing criticism yet again for showing her support for

Japanese Americans. The site of the camp is not currently open to the public.

Poston War Relocation Center was also in Arizona, and was located on the Colorado River Indian Reservation. The tribal council strongly objected to having a prison camp on its land, not wanting to be part of such an injustice. With more than seventeen thousand internees, Poston was the largest of the camps, but its location was so remote that even people living in the area had trouble finding it. The heat in the Sonoran Desert could be extreme. Frequent dust storms added to internees' misery, as did rattlesnakes and scorpions, which were everywhere.

A new arrival wrote: "Extreme heat that can melt iron. No trees, no flowers, no birds singing, not even the sound of an insect, sandy dust whirled into the sky, completely taking the sunshine and light from us." Access to the site of the camp is currently restricted.

The two camps built in Arkansas, **Rohwer War Relocation Center** and **Jerome War Relocation Center**, were just twenty-seven miles apart and were constructed on Mississippi River swampland. In both camps, extreme heat, humidity, and heavy rains were common, and so were poisonous snakes and mosquitoes. Internees suffered from malaria, typhoid fever, and influenza.

An internee said: "When the rains came in Rohwer, we could not leave our quarters. The water stagnated at the front steps. . . . The mosquitos . . . were horrible, and the authorities never had enough quinine for sickness. . . . Rohwer was a living nightmare."

Jerome was the first of the ten permanent camps to close. In June 1944 internees were transferred to other camps and Jerome became a facility for German prisoners of war. Today, Jerome is private farming land. A marker on the site notes its history. At Rohwer, visitors can take a self-guided walking tour and see a monument to internees who lost their lives serving in the 442nd during World War II.

Like all the camps, **Minidoka War Relocation Center** in Idaho was initially a shock for internees. One said: "When we first arrived here we almost cried, and thought that this is the land God had forgotten. The vast expanse of nothing but sagebrush and dust, a landscape so alien to our eyes, and [we experienced] a desolate, woebegone feeling of being so far removed from home and fireside."

In the beginning, the camp had neither hot water for showers nor a sewer system. Internees had to use outdoor latrines. They gathered sagebrush to burn during the cold winters. Summers were dusty, dry, and very hot. Today, the National Park Service operates Minidoka as a historic site. Each summer a Civil Liberties Symposium is held in conjunction with the annual Minidoka Pilgrimage. Visiting attendees learn about the camp's history and then gather to discuss its relevance to current events.

Central Utah War Relocation Center, known as **Topaz**, was 125 miles southwest of Salt Lake City. Area farmers welcomed the camp, hoping for workers to help at harvest time. Unlike at the other camps, internees were almost all from one place: the San Francisco Bay Area. Like the prisoners at Amache, they had more freedom than at other camps. They were allowed to picnic in the desert, go camping, and swim in a nearby swimming hole. They created a library with newspapers and periodicals, plus thousands of books, most sent by outside friends. Materials were available in both English and Japanese. They also created an art school, a literary magazine, and an outstanding camp newspaper.

One artist said, "We will survive if we forget the sands at our feet and look to the mountains for inspiration." The site of the camp is today a national historic landmark. In 2015 the Topaz Museum opened in nearby Delta, Utah, to share the camp's history and stories.

Experiencing Heart Mountain Today

Visitors to the Heart Mountain Interpretive Center (*http://heartmoun tain.org*) on the site of the **Heart Mountain War Relocation Center** are surprised by its size, its open skies, and its namesake mountain on the horizon. The interpretive center's exhibits tell through photos, videos, and testimonies what everyday life was like in the camp. Buildings include an old barracks and one of the massive root cellars where crops were stored. Also on the site are remnants of the hospital, a guard tower, and a memorial dedicated to the Heart Mountain men who served in the war. At the memorial brick pavilion in front of the interpretive center there is a brick inscribed by Norman Mineta in honor of his father.

Attendees at the annual summer three-day Heart Mountain Pilgrimage meet former internees and their descendants and experience a variety of programs, exhibits, and special entertainment. Weather permitting, there's a group outing to climb Heart Mountain. Nearby Cody is home to the Buffalo Bill Center of the West (*https://centerof thewest.org*), an affiliate of the Smithsonian Institution. Close by is Yellowstone National Park.

Visiting Special Places to Learn More

Internet sites such as *https://savingplaces.org/stories/explore-these-west-coast-asian-american-heritage-sites* will suggest places of interest to visit to learn more about Japanese American history. Here are a few of the many to consider:

A ferryboat ride from Seattle, **Bainbridge Island** is home to a powerful memorial honoring islanders who were incarcerated. The Japanese American Exclusion Memorial (*http://bijaema.org*) is a 276-foot-long wall that unfolds like waves and is inscribed with the names of the 276 Japanese Americans who lived on the island. The memorial's tranquil site encourages reflection, as does the wall's inscription: *Nidoto Nai Yoni*—Let It Not Happen Again. Close by is the Bainbridge Island Historical Museum (*http://bainbridgehistory.org*), where knowledgeable volunteers share the island's story. Photos and exhibits bring it to life. One section explores how Japanese Americans stayed connected to their island neighbors during the war, and the role of Walt and Milly Woodward, the editors of the island newspaper.

Little Tokyo in downtown Los Angeles (*http://www.visitlittle tokyo.com*) was once home to thirty thousand Japanese Americans. Today it is one of the few remaining Japantowns in America and is a thriving historic area where visitors can learn about the evacuation of its residents to internment camps, and visit a Japanese garden, Buddhist temples, and a monument to the 442nd Regimental Combat Team. Central to Little Tokyo is the Japanese American National Museum (*http://www.janm.org*), where exhibits tell the story of Japanese American history with an emphasis on their experiences in World War II. Of special interest is a reconstructed barracks from Heart Mountain.

The National Japanese American Memorial to Patriotism *(https://njamemorial.org/)* sits near the White House in Washington, D.C. In Japanese culture the crane symbolizes hope and resilience, and the memorial features a tall pedestal topped by two cranes caught in barbed wire. Quotes from Norman Mineta and other dignitaries, the names of the ten internment camps, and a listing of the eight hundred Japanese American soldiers who died in the war are part of this memorial, which was dedicated in 2000.

Visitors to **San Jose's Japantown** can tour the Japanese American Museum of San Jose (*http://www.jamsj.org*). Rotating exhibits recount the history and contributions of the Japanese immigrants who settled in the area. Museum forums focus on discussions of race, identity, and civil liberties.

Multimedia Recommendations

Books about Japanese American Internment

For Young Readers

NONFICTION

Farewell to Manzanar by Jeanne Wakatsuki Houston and James D. Houston is a memoir of Mrs. Houston's childhood experience in the camp and how incarceration affected members of her family for the rest of their lives.

Life in a Japanese American Internment Camp by Diane Yancey is a fact-filled explanation of what happened and why, and what daily life was like in the camps.

I Am an American by Jerry Stanley is the story of an internee at Manzanar set against the larger history of Japanese Americans.

FICTION

In *Paper Wishes* by Lois Sepahban, ten-year-old Manami and her family must try to deal with the reality of life in an internment camp. Told from Manami's point of view, this story encourages readers to imagine the experience for themselves.

Under the Blood-Red Sun by Graham Salisbury, and his companion work, *Eyes of the Emperor,* combine actual events and people with fictional storytelling to introduce readers to two Hawaiian boys with Japanese ancestry. The first must deal with Pearl Harbor and its aftermath, and the second experiences life in the U.S. Army after Pearl Harbor.

For Older Readers

NONFICTION

Prisoners Without Trial: Japanese Americans in World War II by Roger Daniels is a well-researched book with in-depth information about Japanese American history.

FICTION

In *The Buddha in the Attic* and *When the Emperor Was Divine*, author Julie Otsuka offers rich insight into the Japanese experience of immigrating to America, from the arrival of five picture brides through the experience of the internment camps.

The adult novel *Hotel on the Corner of Bitter and Sweet* by Jamie Ford tells the story of a Chinese American boy named Henry as he observes the evacuation of Seattle's Japanese Americans in 1942, including his special friend, Keiko, and how he revisits this history forty years later.

Additional Recommended Websites

Dedicated to preserving the history of Japanese American incarceration during World War II, Densho—meaning "to pass on to the next generation" in Japanese—is home to the stories and testimonies of those who lived through it (*https://densho.org*). Particularly helpful on the website is an encyclopedia of information about the internment experience and history. An analysis of films and documentaries that depict the internment camp experience in films and documentaries is at *encyclopedia.densho.org/ Dramatic_films/videos_on_incarceration/*.

The Go for Broke National Education Center (*goforbroke.org*) offers education about the special role the 442nd Regimental Combat Team played in World War II. It seeks to promote the virtues and spirit of the soldiers of the 442nd.

The National Park Service (*https://nps.gov*) maintains information on the internment camps.

The official website of the Smithsonian Institution (*Smithsonian.org*) contains a wealth of information about World War II and the incarceration of Japanese Americans. To explore its offerings, enter "Japanese Americans" in the search box.

Searches on YouTube will yield a variety of offerings, some very good, featuring Norman Mineta, Alan Simpson, and Heart Mountain and all the other camps.

Researching This Book

That day I first visited the Heart Mountain Interpretive Center and learned what had happened in that place, I felt an overwhelming anger toward the American government for sending Japanese Americans to prison camps. I also felt gratitude that government officials apologized for this mistake forty-three years after the war ended, and that camp survivors then still alive also received reparations.

When I learned about Norman Mineta and the role he played in making this happen, I wanted to write his story. I couldn't find contact information for him on the Internet but was able to reach him through an association he is affiliated with. When we spoke by phone he told me he had turned down book requests in the past but was saying yes to me because I write for young readers and he wanted them to know the story of America's internment camps.

Two months later I traveled from my home in Kansas City to Norm's home on the Chesapeake Bay near Washington, D.C., to interview him. To prepare, I had read dozens of books—history, biography, memoir—and watched movies and documentaries, all related to World War II and the Japanese American experience. It was helpful that I had spent time in Japan a few years earlier and was acquainted with Japanese culture.

Norm and his wife, Deni, warmly welcomed me to their lovely home and Norm and I settled in at their kitchen table, my tape recorder between us. Beside it was my notebook full of questions. For the next four days we worked. Deni kept us well fed and Norm kept us plied with coffee. When I returned home, I eagerly tackled the project, knowing I had a remarkable story to write.

A little further into the project I interviewed Alan Simpson, who kept me laughing with his salty humor and funny stories. He also shared the sober side of what he had witnessed at Heart Mountain and the challenges of getting the Civil Liberties Act passed in 1988.

Later I visited the Japanese American National Museum in Los Angeles to explore its exhibits and to examine books, documents, and newspapers in its archives. I took copious notes related to Norm's time in Congress and the newspaper coverage of Japanese Americans during the war. When I returned to the Heart Mountain Interpretive Center the following summer, I spent time in its archives reviewing photos that would help to tell the book's story.

During a visit to Bainbridge Island in Washington State I explored the small, splendid island history museum with an island resident who had been sent to Manzanar as a child.

Best of all, in July of 2015 I attended the three-day Heart Mountain Pilgrimage, meeting up with Norm, Deni, and Alan and his wife, Ann. For Norm, the annual event is a reunion with other Nisei who were interned at Heart Mountain. They have a deep bond with one another and are committed to helping preserve the site of the camp and its history so that younger generations can never forget what happened there. All of us in attendance wanted to explore the meaning of the internment experience, to honor those who had been interned, and to memorialize this terrible injustice.

I have felt the weight of what happened to Japanese Americans while writing this book. My hope is that it will help inspire readers to work for liberty and justice for all. We each have the power to make a difference.

Bibliography

Asahina, Robert. *Just Americans: How Japanese Americans Won a War at Home and Abroad.* New York: Gotham Books, 2006.

Cahan, Richard, and Michael Williams. *Un-American: The Incarceration of Japanese Americans During World War II: Images by Dorothea Lange, Ansel Adams, and Other Government Photographers.* Chicago: CityFiles, 2016.

Daniels, Roger. *Prisoners Without Trial: Japanese Americans in World War II.* New York: Hill and Wang, 2004.

Ford, Jamie. *Hotel on the Corner of Bitter and Sweet.* New York: Ballantine Books, 2009.

Fukuda, Curt, and Ralph M. Pearce. *San Jose Japantown: A Journey.* San Jose: Japanese American Museum of San Jose, 2014.

Goodwin, Doris Kearns. *No Ordinary Time: Franklin and Eleanor Roosevelt: The Home Front in World War II.* New York: Simon & Schuster, 1994.

Gordon, Linda, and Gary Y. Okihiro. *Impounded: Dorothea Lange and the Censored Images of Japanese American Internment.* New York: W. W. Norton, 2006.

Hardy, Donald Loren. *Shooting from the Lip: The Life of Senator Al Simpson.* Norman: University of Oklahoma Press, 2011.

Houston, Jeanne Wakatsuki, and James D. Houston. *Farewell to Manzanar: A True Story of Japanese American Experience During and After the World War II Internment.* New York: Ember / Random House, 2012.

Lee, Erika. *The Making of Asian America: A History.* New York: Simon & Schuster, 2015.

Mackey, Mike. *Heart Mountain: Life in Wyoming's Concentration Camp.* Powell, WY: Western History Publications, 2000.

McGaugh, Scott. *Honor Before Glory: The Epic World War II Story of the Japanese American GIs Who Rescued the Lost Battalion.* Philadelphia: Da Capo, 2016.

McKay, Susan. *The Courage Our Stories Tell: The Daily Lives and Maternal Child Health Care of Japanese American Women at Heart Mountain.* Powell, WY: Western History Publications, 2002.

Nakagawa, Kerry Yo. *Through a Diamond: 100 Years of Japanese American Baseball.* San Francisco: Rudi Publishing, 2001.

Oppenheim, Joanne. *Dear Miss Breed: True Stories of the Japanese American Incarceration During World War II and a Librarian Who Made a Difference.* New York: Scholastic, 2006.

Otsuka, Julie. *The Buddha in the Attic.* New York: Anchor Books, 2011.

—————. *When the Emperor Was Divine.* New York: Anchor Books, 2003.

Reeves, Richard. *Infamy: The Shocking Story of the Japanese American Internment in World War II.* New York: Henry Holt, 2015.

Salisbury, Graham. *Eyes of the Emperor.* New York: Random House Children's Books, 2005.

—————. *Under the Blood-Red Sun.* New York: Delacorte Press, 1994.

Sepahban, Lois. *Paper Wishes.* New York: Farrar Straus Giroux, 2016.

Stanley, Jerry. *I Am an American: A True Story of Japanese Internment.* New York: Crown, 1994.

Woodward, Mary. *In Defense of Our Neighbors: The Walt and Milly Woodward Story.* Bainbridge Island, WA: Fenwick Publishing, 2008.

Yancey, Diane. *Life in a Japanese American Internment Camp.* San Diego, CA: Lucent Books, 1998.

Zinn, Howard. *A People's History of the United States 1492–Present.* New York: HarperPerennial, 1995.

Notes

Epigraphs

    p. ix "I want my children to understand": Barbara Yasui, "Sensei Perspective," Kokoro Kara, newsletter of the Heart Mountain Wyoming Foundation, summer 2015, p. 8.

    p. ix "we carried Strength, Dignity, and Soul": "Only What We Can Carry Project," Bainbridge Island School District No. 303, *https://www.bisd303.org/Page/5606.*

Chapter 4: The World at War

    p. 33 "A viper is nonetheless a viper wherever the egg is hatched": Stanley, p. 18.

    p. 34 "must not feel they have suddenly ceased to be Americans": Goodwin, p. 297.

Chapter 5: Lowering the Net

    p. 36 When one Japanese American in the Seattle area: Mackey, p. 2.

    p. 39 "We're charged with wanting to get rid of the Japanese": Cahan and Williams, p. 57.

Chapter 6: Losing Everything

    p. 45 One Bainbridge evacuee recounted: Woodward, p. 70.

Chapter 10: New Routines

p. 94 "We heard this poor voice, almost choking with tears": Reeves, p. 139.

Chapter 12: Baseball!

p. 108 "Hey, Tojo!": Nakagawa, p. 93.

Chapter 13: Meeting the Enemy

p. 116 "have a dislike for any Orientals": Reeves, p. 98.

p. 118 "It was strange how the internees were great people": Mackey, p. 90.

Chapter 17: Going Home

p. 153 Soon the family was back in business: Woodward, p. 115.

p. 155 "These disgraceful incidents": Reeves, p. 267.

Chapter 19: A Distinguished Career

p. 171 "race prejudice, war hysteria, and a failure of political leadership": Reeves, p. 276.

p. 172 "Would I sell my civil and constitutional rights": Daniels, p. 102.

p. 172 "Our own government had branded us": Chris Komai, "Norman Mineta: A Lifetime of Public Service," May 23, 2012, Discover Nikkei, www.discovernikkei.org/en/journal/2012/5/23/norman-mineta/.

p. 173 "We can never fully right the wrongs of the past": Yancey, p. 96.

Additional Information

p. 185 "All we could see was sand": Woodward, p. 76.

p. 185 "We slept in the dust, we breathed the dust": Yancey, p. 47.

p. 187 "Extreme heat that can melt iron": Reeves, p. 108.

p. 188 "When the rains came in Rohwer": "Rohwer," Densho Encyclopedia, encyclopedia.densho.org/Rohwer/.

p. 188 "When we first arrived here we almost cried": "Japanese American Incarceration during World War II," Friends of Minidoka, http://www.minidoka.org/history-world-war-two-internment.

p. 189 "We will survive if we forget the sands": "Topaz," Densho Encyclopedia, http://encyclopedia.densho.org/Topaz/.

Photo Credits

Bainbridge Island Japanese American Community: p. 44

The Bancroft Library, University of California, Berkeley. War Relocation Authority photographs [graphic]: Japanese-American evacuation and resettlement, BANC PIC 1967.014: p. 61 (WRA no. A-142 [recto]), p. 101 (WRA no. E-591), p. 157 (WRA no. I-101), p. 182 (WRA no. -905)

Buffalo Bill Center of the West, Cody, Wyoming, U.S.A.; Jack Richard Collection: p. 113 (PN.89.107.21020.02.3), p. 125 (PN.89.111.21235.1)

California History Room, California State Library, Sacramento, California: p. 17

California State Parks: Image 090-706: p. 18

California State University Japanese American Digitization Project: p. 66

Dell Family Collection: p. 83

Estelle Ishigo Collection, American Heritage Center, University of Wyoming: pp. 90, 91, 93

Frank Abe: p. 142

George and Frank C. Hirahara Photograph Collection, 1943–1945, Manuscripts, Archives and Special Collections, Washington State University Libraries: p. 103 bottom (Image sc14b01f0105n07.jpg, collection no. SC 14)

History San José: p. 48 (inset of instruction notice)

Japanese American National Museum: p. 107 (Gift of Mori Shimada, 92.10.2A), p. 109 (Gift of Mori Shimada, 92.10.2E)

Kinoshita Family Collection: p. 173

Library of Congress: p.15 (LC-DIG-ggbain-12867), pp. 31, 49 (LC-USF34-T01-072263-D), p. 50 (LC-DIG-ppmsca-38736), p. 52 (LC-DIG-fsa-8a31149), p. 53 (LC-USF33-013290-M1), p. 57 (LC-USF34-072349-D), p. 60 (LC-USF33-013298-M3), p. 74 (LC-USZ62-133633), p. 137 (LC-USW3-012125-C), p. 147 (LC-USZ62-36452), p. 163 (LC-DIG-ppprs-00421), p. 170 (LC-USZ62-139501), p. 177 (Photo by Jane Sargus)

Museum of History & Industry, Seattle; Seattle Post-Intelligencer Collection: p. 37 (number PI-28032), p. 154 (number PI-28084)

The National Archives and Records Administration: pp. 24, 32 (210-G-C449), p. 41 (520053), p. 43 (210-G-B77), p. 45 (210-G-A530), p. 46 (210-G-C141), p. 47, p. 48 (street scene), p. 58 (210-G-B414), p. 59 (210-G-B388), p. 62 (210-G-C23), p. 64 (210-G-C80), p. 79 (210-G-E134), p. 80 (210-G-E727), p. 82 (210-G-E99), p. 85 (27813708), p. 86 (210-G-E677), p. 100 (210-G-B570), p. 103 top (210-G-G202), p. 104 (210-G-E927), p. 105 (210-G-I65), pp. 117, 124 (210-G-E101), p. 126 (210-G-G217), p. 155 (210-G-K374), p. 158 (210-G-G945), p. 187

National Baseball Hall of Fame and Museum, Cooperstown, N.Y.: p. 110 (Ruth Babe _5487-88 _w Gehrig Grp_NBL.jpg)

Norman Mineta: pp. ii, 7, 8, 11, 19, 20, 128, 161, 162, 164, 167, 175

Ralph Pearce: p. 22

Seattle Nisei Veterans Committee and the U.S. Army: p. 144

Smithsonian National Air and Space Museum: p. 114 (NASM 00186615)

Theodore Akimoto Family Collection: p. 150

University of California San Diego Library, Special Collection & Archives: p. 29

U.S. Senate Historical Office: p. 171

Wyoming State Archives: p. 115

Yoshio Okumoto: pp. 78, 81, 89, 98, 99, 122, 127

Acknowledgments

First and foremost, my thanks to Norman Mineta for sharing his story with me and for his patience and cheerfulness as I asked endless questions both in person and in phone conversations. Peggy Klappenberger, where would I have been without your calm, steady help as Norm's assistant? Thank you! And Deni Mineta, thank you for your gracious hospitality. Thanks, also, to Alan Simpson for so willingly taking the time to work with me—testimony to his deep friendship with Norm—and to his assistant, Ann Pendley, for helping in various ways.

As always I am grateful to my longtime agent, Regina Ryan, who even went to visit Heart Mountain to see it for herself. And thanks to these folks for major assistance: Dakota Russell, Deborah Shouse, Barbara Bartocci, Kym Wiedenkeller, Pat McNees, Greg Schultz, Ralph Pearce, Patti McCracken, and Kerry Yo Nakagawa. Sandy Lamb, it was a pleasure exploring Heart Mountain and Bainbridge Island with you. Kristin von Kreisler, thanks for welcoming me to your island home and showing me the memorial. I am also grateful to Alison Doerr and Kaden Doerr for accompanying me to Little Tokyo and the Japanese American National Museum and for understanding my hectic work schedule. Finally, my thanks to Margaret Ferguson and all the folks at Holiday House for seeing the potential in this story and enthusiastically shepherding this book to publication.

Index

Note: Page references in *italic* refer to photographs.